Unlocking
Speakin[g]
Listen

Also available:

Unlocking Creativity
Teaching Across the Curriculum
Edited by Robert Fisher and Mary Williams
1-84312-092-5

Unlocking Literacy
Second edition
Edited by Robert Fisher and Mary Williams
1-84312-386-X

Unlocking Learning and Teaching with ICT
Identifying and Overcoming Barriers
Helena Gillespie
1-84312-376-2

Unlocking Speaking and Listening

Edited by
Pamela Hodson and Deborah Jones

 David Fulton Publishers

David Fulton Publishers Ltd
The Chiswick Centre, 414 Chiswick High Road, London W4 5TF

www.fultonpublishers.co.uk

First published in Great Britain in 2006 by David Fulton Publishers

10 9 8 7 6 5 4 3 2 1

David Fulton Publishers is a division of Granada Learning Limited.

British Library Cataloguing in Publication Data
A catalogue record for this book is available from the British Library.

ISBN: 1 84312 392 4

Typeset by FiSH Books, Enfield, Middlesex
Printed and bound in Great Britain

Contents

Acknowledgements

We would particularly like to thank the following children whose talk has inspired us to produce this book: Evan, Cerys and Dylan Jones, Andrew Turner, James Fox, Gemma Paine, Harriet and James Taylor, Joshua Nagel, Daniel Rosenberg, Sophie and James Cobley.

We would also like to thank the students of Brunel University who have worked with us as co-researchers and provided fresh insights into developing speaking and listening in the classroom context.

About the contributors

Alastair Daniel studied mime and physical theatre and ran a touring company for three and a half years. Following this, he spent four years teaching dance, drama, religious education and maths and also worked as a language support teacher. He currently describes himself as a 'roving educator' and his storytelling and teaching have taken him to many countries, including The Netherlands, Belgium, China and the USA. Alastair is currently engaged in doctoral research in performance theory and leads a storytelling module on the BA Primary English course at Kingston University.
Website: www.storytent.co.uk

Yota Dimitriadi is a lecturer in ICT in Education at Reading University. She was formerly a Senior Lecturer at Kingston University and a research associate for Special Educational Needs Joint Initiative for Training (SENJIT) at the Institute of Education, University of London. She chairs the ICT and Inclusion Experts Panel of the British Computer Society. Her past experience includes working as a secondary English teacher before moving to the British Dyslexia Association. Her research interests have focused on the use of technology for SEN and EAL children. She has presented her work on inclusion, multilingualism and the new technologies at a number of national and international conferences. She received an award for her work at the CAL conference in 1999 and 2003. In 2003, with Pam Hodson, she received a Becta research bursary to develop a project on digital video with multilingual children with special needs.

Robert Fisher is a teacher, writer and researcher on teaching thinking, learning and creativity. His books include *Teaching Children to Think, Teaching Children to Learn, Stories for Thinking* (Nash Pollock), *Poems for Thinking, Games for Thinking, Values for Thinking, Teaching Thinking* (Continuum) and *Head Start*, and he is general editor of the *Unlocking…* series published by Fulton. His PhD was awarded for research on philosophy with children. He works part-time as

Professor of Education at Brunel University, and as a consultant to many professional development projects and keynote presenter at national and international conferences focusing on creativity, dialogic teaching and personalised learning.
Website: www.teachingthinking.net

Nicola Grove is a Senior Lecturer in the Department of Language and Communication Science at City University, London. She has contributed to many initiatives concerned with inclusion and the National Curriculum, including the development of P-scales, target setting materials and, most recently, inclusion resources to support the delivery of speaking, listening and learning. She is currently on secondment to the British Institute of Learning Disabilities, directing a project to train people with learning disabilities as community storytellers. Her publications include *Ways into Literature* (Jessica Kingsley), *Odyssey Now* (David Fulton Publishers) and *Augmentative and Alternative Communication: Developmental Issues*, edited with Stephen von Tetzchner (Whurr Publishers).
Website: www.storytracks.com

Pamela Hodson is currently a principal lecturer at Kingston University where she is subject leader for primary English. Formerly at Brunel University, she was also Head of the English Department in a large mixed comprehensive school in Richmond upon Thames. She worked as an advisory teacher for three years on the LINC (Language in the National Curriculum) project and is co-author, with Deborah Jones, of *Teaching Children to Write: The Process Approach to Writing for Literacy* (David Fulton Publishers). She has collaborated with Yota Dimitriadi on a Becta-funded research project to explore how digital video can support the literacy development of multilingual children with special needs.

Colleen Johnson spent several years as an actor in Canada and the UK, working mainly in theatre in education, co-founding two theatre companies. She has a wide range of teaching experience, specialising in drama, voice production and lecturing skills. Previously at Brunel University, she is a Senior Lecturer in Drama in Primary Education at St Mary's University College, Twickenham.

Deborah Jones has been a primary teacher and LEA advisory teacher and has worked on the LINC project. She is currently a Senior Lecturer in Brunel University and teaches on postgraduate, master's and doctoral programmes. Her research interests include literacy and gender in education. She co-authored with Pamela Hodson *Teaching Children to Write* (David Fulton Publishers).

Ruth Lewis has taught pupils with EAL in primary, secondary and early years classrooms for over 20 years, first, as a class teacher and later as an advisory teacher. For the past 15 years, she has worked for the Hounslow Language Service where she has been responsible for training undergraduates, teachers and overseas trained teachers. Her work has taken her to Africa. Her publications include *Guidelines for Class Teachers: Working with Beginners in English* and its accompanying, award-winning video.

Geeta Ludhra currently co-ordinates the Literacy and Gifted and Talented strand in teaching and learning within a multicultural school in Southall. She has also worked as a leading literacy teacher and is a guest lecturer on the PGCE Primary English programme at Brunel University.

Hilma Rask taught in London primary schools for a number of years, and also taught English as a Foreign Language to adults in both Finland and England. As an advisory teacher, she established and managed the work of a primary language support team in the London Borough of Richmond upon Thames. She spent nine years as a lecturer in Primary Education at Brunel University, where she taught on ITT, PGCE, and Master's level courses. Her special interests include international and comparative education, early years education and language and literacy. Hilma currently works as a freelance education consultant and researcher.

Mary Williams taught for 20 years as a primary school teacher, the last nine as head teacher of a nursery/infant school. She is a part-time Senior Research Fellow at Brunel University with research interests that include literacy learning, educating pupils in the early years and metacognition. She also works for the Brunel Able Children's centre as a freelance education consultant. She is co-editor of *Unlocking Literacy, Unlocking Creativity* and editor of *Unlocking Writing* (David Fulton Publishers).

Introduction

I really like talking. It helps me think things through. I love it when we get the chance to talk about our work.

(William, aged 8)

It is evident that most children love to talk. Traditionally, however, perceptions of talk in an educational context have been negative. A noisy classroom was synonymous with loss of teacher control; a quiet classroom indicative of productive work. Whereas recent initiatives have sought to redress this, many teachers, although convinced of the value of speaking and listening, still remain insecure about how to use talk effectively within the teaching and learning process.

The National Literacy Strategy (DfEE 1998) has had a significant impact on teaching and learning styles in the classroom. Much of the emphasis has been on teacher-focused and teacher-directed talk, with children having few opportunities to extend their spoken language in a structured, systematic way. In 2003, *Excellence and Enjoyment* advocated a more flexible approach to teaching and, read in conjunction with the guidance on speaking and listening (DfES 2003), set the scene for enabling teachers to reappraise their practice. Although the guidance provides some valuable ideas for teaching speaking and listening, teachers have not significantly changed their approaches.

It is our view that in order to wholeheartedly embrace the effective teaching of speaking and listening, teachers need to have a rationale, a clear understanding of why they should do it, as well as how they should do it. Our experience of working on the LINC (Language in the Curriculum, 1989–92) project convinced us that teachers' practice can only be enhanced when underpinned by sound subject knowledge and a rigorous theoretical base. This book, therefore, aims to provide practical strategies for planning, teaching and assessing speaking and listening. Throughout, this is supported by theory and research that will enhance teachers' subject knowledge.

In Chapter 1, Pamela Hodson contextualises current educational theory and practice in relation to speaking and listening. She considers why teachers are reluctant to embrace recent guidance in the teaching of this key area. Drawing on her own recent research together with research carried out in Australia, she presents practical ideas for the effective teaching of speaking and listening in the classroom. The chapter provides a rationale for what follows in the rest of the book.

Chapter 2 focuses on speaking and listening in the Foundation Stage of education. Hilma Rask emphasises the critical role of the teacher as both active listener and an expert companion in dialogue with children. She draws on observations from classroom experience to highlight how purposeful Speaking and Listening can support children's learning in an early years setting.

Robert Fisher advocates an approach called Philosophy for Children that emphasises the development of children's critical thinking through questioning and dialogue in the classroom context. Chapter 3 is about a special form of 'talking to think' which not only helps children's communication skills, but also develops habits of intelligent behaviour.

In Chapter 4, Nicola Grove considers the challenges facing teachers in supporting SEN children in speaking and listening. She addresses these issues within the wider concept of communication and presents practical strategies for inclusive practice in mainstream classrooms. Using a case study approach, she illustrates a range of special educational needs. She advocates a pedagogical approach that supports all children and recognises the interaction between context, communication and the learner. If this is the case, she suggests, it will be easier to identify the pupils who need extra provision to meet their individual needs.

Alastair Daniel explores the essential role of the teacher as a principal classroom storyteller. In Chapter 5, he sets out to show that by experiencing imaginative storytelling, children are not only inspired to become creative and confident storytellers in their own right, but can also become active and comprehending listeners. This chapter is concerned with identifying the essential elements of effective storytelling and how to develop teachers' confidence and skills across the curriculum.

Chapter 6 considers the key role of speaking and listening as it relates to gifted and talented children. Drawing on findings from a DfES project 'Nurturing Young Talent', Mary Williams identifies how higher ability pupils need to be motivated through challenging activities that promote deep levels of thinking. She emphasises the inter-relationship of speaking, listening, reading and writing to show how children's potential in oracy can be utilised to the full. Practical ways of challenging and stimulating higher ability pupils are suggested.

In Chapter 7, Colleen Johnson discusses how drama can present an unlimited range of contexts in which children can experience diversity and spoken language. She identifies the fact that although drama practitioners may welcome the re-emergence of drama in the primary curriculum, teachers entering the profession in the past decade may well lack confidence in this area. Her chapter, therefore, provides practical strategies for the non-specialist which can be incorporated within lessons such as literacy and personal, social and moral education.

Chapter 8 highlights the need to embed the planning, teaching and assessment of speaking and listening in the everyday routines of the primary classroom. Deborah Jones demonstrates an awareness of the complexity of assessing speaking and listening and acknowledges that teachers find this a challenging area. The chapter, therefore, presents practical strategies for promoting children's development and shows how evidence of progression in this area can be harnessed and recorded.

Ways of supporting EAL learners are suggested by Ruth Lewis in Chapter 9. Again, the critical role of the teacher in both modelling and scaffolding Speaking and Listening is emphasised. The need to provide a welcoming classroom environment that celebrates linguistic diversity is described as an effective starting point. She draws on work carried out by the Hounslow Language Service and presents a range of approaches, such as the use of key visuals, for implementation in the classroom.

The role and potential of technology in supporting children's Speaking and Listening development are discussed in the final chapter. Yota Dimitriadi, Pamela Hodson and Geeta Ludhra draw upon a range of case studies where technology (from the use of the humble tape recorder to new technologies such as digital video, voice-activated software and programmable toys) is used to extend children's exploratory talk. The book, therefore, concludes with a focus on the new technologies and points the way forward for future contexts for developing children's Speaking and Listening.

CHAPTER 1

Listening to children's voices: unlocking speaking and listening in the primary classroom

Pamela Hodson

Talking in school is very important – you need to be able to ask questions, get along with your friends and talk about your feelings. We also talk when we're doing investigations in science, such as discussing which melts the fastest – ice or chocolate. And the best thing is – we get to eat the chocolate!

(Gemma, age 9)

Although Gemma might rank eating chocolate more highly than speaking and listening in the classroom, this quotation demonstrates how children can readily identify some of the different kinds of talk that occur in the classroom – both social and cognitive. In Gemma's school, the development of children's spoken language is considered key to underpinning their learning in all areas of the curriculum and is valued by teachers and children alike. This reflects the views expressed in the first English National Curriculum (DfES 1988) that the inclusion of speaking and listening as a separate profile component, and, indeed, the first profile component, demonstrates a conviction that children's speaking and listening skills are central to children's development.[1] Literature also provides us with a striking example of the value of spoken communication. When Billy Casper, the normally reticent, much-bullied, adolescent central character in *A Kestrel for a Knave*,[2] is given the opportunity to speak about his passion, his kestrel, in front of the class, an articulate expert is revealed. Children are empowered by having a voice in the classroom, but recent initiatives such as the Literacy and Numeracy Strategies have not always fostered this approach. Indeed, Robin Alexander (2005) has gone so far as to suggest that these strategies have actually promoted low level classroom interactions which are cognitively unchallenging.[3] Recent documents such as *Speaking, Listening, Learning* (DfES 2003b) and *Excellence and Enjoyment* (DfES 2003a) would seem to advocate a classroom approach which reaffirms the fundamental role that language plays in children's learning and encourages a more flexible, creative approach to literacy teaching.

This chapter will aim to put into context the new guidance on speaking and listening – *Speaking, Listening, Learning: Working with Children in Key Stages 1 and 2* (DfES 2003b) – and consider ways to implement its recommendations in the classroom. The teaching of speaking and listening has always been a richly controversial and much debated field and its re-emergence as being central to children's learning and literacy development also brings to the fore complex and challenging issues, not least in reappraising the way in which literacy is taught in the classroom.

Current context

In 1988, the Cox Report stated that the value of talk as a means of learning was widely accepted. However, it is true to say that for the past ten years, while there has been a firm emphasis on raising standards in reading and writing in primary schools, the explicit teaching of speaking and listening has been neglected. The National Literacy Strategy (DfEE 1998), which has had a very significant impact on how English is taught in the primary classroom, acknowledges the role that oral work plays in children's literacy development, yet its many objectives address mainly reading and writing. Aspects of speaking and listening are implicit: 'Literacy…also involves speaking and listening which, although they are not separately identified in the framework, are an essential part of it' (DfEE 1998: 3). The words 'discuss' and 'summarise orally' do appear, but the strategy's drive has been focused on the teaching of reading and writing and classroom practice has reflected this.

In 2003, as a result of a partnership between the QCA and the National Literacy Strategy, in response to a perceived need for support from teachers, new guidelines were developed to raise the profile of speaking and listening in the primary classroom (DfES 2003b) As the guidance highlights, its aim is to complement the strategy's objectives for reading and writing and to reflect the National Curriculum programmes of study for speaking and listening both in English and across the curriculum.

Background to speaking and listening

National initiatives for the development of speaking and listening are not new. In 1987, the National Oracy Project was established to enhance the role of speaking and listening in the learning process by improving children's performance across the curriculum and encouraging active learning.[4] The late 1980s and early 1990s proved to be an extremely rich era in teaching where the profile of speaking and listening was high and debate about it was fierce. In addition to the National Oracy Project, the LINC Project (Language in the National Curriculum, 1989–92) was designed to support teachers' knowledge and understanding of language in order to implement the effective introduction of the National Curriculum. Unlike the National Literacy Strategy, the LINC project did not set out to give teachers guidance on how to teach. The project proved to be highly controversial with government and politicians, but highly successful with many teachers. Influences from both of these projects can be seen in the new guidance on speaking and listening.

Speaking, Listening, Learning: Working with Children in Key Stages 1 and 2 and the National Curriculum

The guidance is related to the four interdependent aspects of speaking and listening in the National Curriculum programmes of study for English (Table 1.1). As its title suggests, the central role of oral language in children's learning is a fundamental aspect of the new guidance in parallel with the desire to raise standards further. It identifies 67 distinct objectives for speaking and listening which are organised in two ways: chronologically, and then divided into the separate key strands of speaking; listening; group discussion and interaction; and drama. The difficulty of presenting any linear model of language is that language development is not linear; it is recursive. To a certain extent, the objectives do reflect this, identifying language skills that are revisited and developed in different years, for example, increasing development of the ability to tell a story and developing confidence and sophistication in operating as an effective member of a group. However, children's progress in speaking and listening will vary tremendously according to each individual, so teachers also face the challenge of setting goals that are achievable and appropriate to the child's language development.

Table 1.1 National Curriculum programmes of study for English

Speaking	Listening	Group discussion and interaction	Drama
Being able to speak clearly and to develop and sustain ideas in talk	Developing active listening strategies and critical skills of analysis	Taking different roles in groups, making a range of contributions and working collaboratively	Improvising and working in role, scripting and performing and responding to performances

The guidance is also linked to key objectives from the Literacy Strategy Framework, for example, Year 3, Term 3, objective 35: 'To use the language of possibility to investigate and reflect on feelings, behaviour or relationships' is linked to the NLS text level objective 5 of the same term: 'To discuss characters' feelings, behaviour, relationships, referring to the text and making judgements'.

Literary texts such as narrative, poetry and drama texts also provide the stimulus for exploration, analysis and discussion in the objectives. In addition, investigating language use and variety in a range of contexts is also embedded in the guidance as well as critical engagement with media texts such as advertisements or TV programmes.

The ways in which speaking and listening can be taught and used as a means of learning in other subject areas are also emphasised. Moral issues discussed in PSHE can be used as way of actively engaging in group work through the resolution of differences by exploring alternative viewpoints, making decisions and justifying choices. PE presents opportunities to describe performance; Science and Maths to use appropriate technical language, ask questions, decide how these can be investigated and explain reasoning. The guidance also highlights the requirement that children should use, where appropriate, standard English; a complex issue which is addressed later in the chapter.

Excellence and Enjoyment

The guidance on speaking and listening needs to be set within the context of *Excellence and Enjoyment: A Strategy for Primary Schools* (DfES 2003a), which appeared in the same year and advocated a more flexible approach to teaching the Literacy Hour. It suggested that schools should be adapting the strategy to meet their own particular needs, highlighting the non-statutory nature of both the Literacy and Numeracy Strategies.[5] In essence, there appeared to be a clear mandate for schools to take ownership of the teaching of the curriculum and adapt it in a more creative fashion.

Responding to the guidance

Has there been a considerable shift in primary classroom practice towards a more balanced approach to teaching speaking and listening, reading and writing? Initial research by Hodson in 2005[6] would seem to indicate that the new guidance has not been universally adopted. At best, schools' and teachers' responses to implementing the guidance have been tentative and practice has been patchy. Some schools have identified that it is not a priority and there is often an assumption that speaking and listening occur 'naturally' and happen implicitly as part of the normal school day. In many instances, teachers demonstrate a suspicion of speaking and listening, fearing that they will 'lose control' and while 'good listening' is often rewarded in the classroom, 'good speaking' is rarely celebrated. Children, too, often seem to perceive talk as something furtive which goes on when the teacher isn't looking or behind a strategically placed hand when you 'get away with it' in assembly. For many children, talk is something that they do in the playground, before lessons begin and something 'you don't do when you need to concentrate when you're learning'. Children's perceptions are not all negative, however, as is evidenced in the opening quotation. In contrast, when children were given opportunities to work in groups, they were able to articulate how talking had helped them to learn. Several children discussed the pleasure they gained from reading and sharing books with their peers and collaborating over a writing task. When engaged in explicit discussion about the nature of talk, children demonstrated insightful perceptions of what makes a good speaker and a good listener and considerable enthusiasm for the topic of speaking and listening as a whole.

Whole-school approach to speaking and listening

For teachers, the guidance presents considerable challenges, not least in generating a change in a classroom ethos which, since the inception of the Literacy Strategy, has focused largely on teacher-led discussion and in promoting a whole-school ethos where speaking and listening is valued. In addition, speaking and listening is an extremely complex and controversial topic. Many teachers face pressure from parents and the media to promote a more traditional view of learning, where a quiet classroom is perceived as the most effective for successful teaching and learning.

However, in Iver Village School in Buckinghamshire, the guidance was a reaffirmation of work they had already started. Stemming from a conviction that children's development in speaking and listening is critical for their social, literacy and cognitive development, speaking and listening had already been identified as key to raising standards in all areas of the curriculum. The whole school were involved in a process of reviewing the curriculum and the following areas were addressed:

- identifying opportunities for speaking and listening in each unit of work;
- using staff meetings and outside agencies to inform teachers' understanding of speaking and listening;
- introducing speaking and listening first into literacy lessons and then into all subjects.

Key to the success of the work at the school was a process of review, innovation and evaluation that involved all the staff. In order to embed speaking and listening, the staff focused on adopting strategies such as using the interactive whiteboard to support 'oral starters' at the beginning of a literacy lesson, where teachers used sentences such as 'Tell me why...' to promote detailed responses from the children. Oral storytelling, performance poetry and formal presentations were integrated into the schemes of work. In order to support the development of children's critical engagement and discursive skills around concepts, the teachers devised a series of sentences related to particular subject areas which would then become an intrinsic part of the topics (Table 1.2).

Table 1.2 Questions to embed critical engagement and discussion

Literacy	Numeracy	History
Topic: Spoken and Written Language	Topic: Subtraction	Topic: The Tudors
• There is no difference between spoken and written language. • Punctuation can replace pauses and gestures. • You have to use whole sentences when you speak, but not when you write. • You can't write down everything you say.	• You can 'count on' to subtract. • Subtracting two odd numbers always makes an even number. • Another way to subtract is to say, 'Find the quotient.' • Knowing my number bonds to ten helps me subtract.	• Tudor people didn't know anything about the rest of the world. • Henry VIII wasn't interested in religion. • Henry VIII was allowed to have six wives because he was king. • What plates were made of tells us if they belonged to rich or poor people.
Topic: Vocabulary Extension	Topic: Multiplication	Topic: Invaders and Settlers
• Technical words are nothing to do with non-fiction writing. • If I write 'He's gone round the bend', I don't mean that he's gone out of sight. • Some words only have one opposite, while others have more than one. • Onomatopoeia means words which echo sounds.	• If I want to multiply by 6, I can multiply by 3, then double. • For some calculations, I halve the smaller number and double the other. • Quotient is the opposite of product. • To make a number square, multiply it by itself.	• Invaders only came to Britain by invitation. • What happened is more important than when it happened. • Nothing is left from the Roman, Viking or Anglo-Saxon invasions.

Source: Devised by Chris Smith and Jane Balgobin, Iver Village Junior School www.speakingthoughts.co.uk

For this school, the new guidance on speaking and listening presented a baseline which they decided to extend and develop further. Their work underlines the complexity of the teaching of speaking and listening and highlights the importance of the role of the teacher. In this context, staff have responded very positively to the initiative and have welcomed the opportunity to vary their teaching styles in the classroom.

The teacher's role

Language acquisition

An understanding of how children acquire language is fundamental to informing how speaking and listening is taught in the classroom and this has been recognised for a long time.[7]

> Andrew, aged 4, was playing with his mother, throwing a ball backwards and forwards.
>
> 'Catch the ball, Andrew!'
> 'I catched the ball!' was the triumphant response as the ball landed in Andrew's arms.
> 'No, say "I caught the ball,"' corrected his mother.
> 'Catched, caught. I'm fed up with this game.'

Andrew's frustration with the apparent inconsistencies of verb construction was evident. However, this example serves to demonstrate that learning language is not merely a process of mimicking adults. Andrew applies known rules of past tense formation, such as adding -ed to the end of the verb, but in this case those rules do not apply. In this context, Andrew's use of language is recognised as a sign of growth, a child's understanding that language is a system and rule-governed, but he has not yet acquired mastery of that system.

Scaffolding children's language

There are clear implications for the crucial role that a teacher plays in building a bridge between the child's current knowledge, what they already know about language, and helping them towards progressively more advanced levels of competence.[8] This makes significant demands on the teacher's knowledge and understanding of each individual child's competence in speaking and listening and highlights the need for effective assessment and rigorous planning in order to provide the child with appropriate scaffolding. As the expert role model for spoken language, teachers also need to present an appropriate model for spoken standard English in the classroom and to present opportunities for children to use and explore appropriate contexts for using standard English. This is an integral part of the National Curriculum programmes of study for speaking and listening and the objectives for speaking and listening.

Standard English

The view adopted by the Working Group for National Curriculum English (1989) that standard English is a social dialect associated with particular uses, especially in areas of power, proved to be highly unpopular among people who wanted it to be viewed as the 'correct' way to talk. The Group stated that standard English was not inherently superior to all other forms of English and highlighted research which demonstrated that all other dialects were rule-governed and systematic, not deviant forms of standard English. For teachers, it is vital to respect the child's home dialect, but it is certainly true to say that not having the ability to use standard English will exclude adults from areas of power, such as government, law, education, commerce and the media. The National Curriculum, English (1999: 17) states that at Key Stage 1 'Pupils should be introduced to some of the main features of spoken standard English and be taught how to use them' progressing through to Key Stage 2 where they 'should be taught the grammatical constructions that are characteristic of spoken standard English and to apply this knowledge in a range of contexts' (p. 29).

Children need to be made aware that standard English can be spoken with any accent (regional newsreaders provide ready-made evidence of this) and that its use is not confined to speakers who may use an accent such as 'Received Pronunciation' or BBC English, as it is sometimes known.

The explicit study of standard English provides a rich resource for language study in the classroom and is most effective when explored in context. Many children, from an early age, demonstrate the ability to change their language according to whom they are with and why they are speaking. Observations of children's self-corrections in whole-class teaching demonstrate this.

A Year 4 class were discussing the actions of the characters in the story they were reading. Anna responded to her teacher's question by stating emphatically, 'He didn't do nothing wrong.' After a moment's pause, she re-stated carefully, 'He didn't do *anything* wrong', with a deliberate emphasis on the 'anything' to underscore her knowledge. In this context, the teacher had allowed time for Anna's self-correction before intervening or re-modelling her response, providing the opportunity for the child to demonstrate her growing proficiency in using language appropriately. This knowledge can be exploited and developed further through role play, formal debates and presentations in the classroom where the appropriate use of standard English can provide both the focus for use and reflection on language usage.

As standard English is the form of language most commonly used in writing, the need to develop children's competence in this area is unquestionable. However, in standard English, there are differences of style, particularly in the continuum between formal and informal language and differences between standard English spoken in different parts of the wider-speaking English world. Most children, used to exposure of films and TV series from the USA and Australia, can readily identify different word usages; the BBC website http://www.bbc.co.uk/voices provides an excellent resource of regional accents and dialects.

Metalanguage and a grammar for talk – the differences between spoken and written language

The guidance highlights the need for children to be taught and to use technical language which is relevant for each subject area. At Key Stages 3 and 4, a document 'Introducing the grammar of talk'[9] discusses and identifies what kind of shared language can be used to describe talk itself. While this may not be wholly appropriate to children in primary schools, it is important that children are made aware of the differences between speech and writing and that speech is not simply a substandard form of writing. The discussion questions on spoken and written language formulated by teachers at Iver School already identified can form the basis for this kind of investigation.

Types of talk in the classroom

Teachers also need to reflect on the kind of speaking and listening that they promote in the classroom. It is evident that there is a significant difference between spoken discourse in the classroom and that in the community outside the classroom. In essence, a lot of classroom practice is typified by the IRF (Initiation, Response, Feedback) or IRE (Initiation, Response, Evaluation) sequence where the teacher initiates talk with a question, children respond, and through the teacher's feedback, the teacher controls the language and meaning and signals what is to be viewed as relevant knowledge within the classroom. This kind of sequence is characteristic of many of the teacher–pupil interchanges which take place during whole-class teaching in the Literacy Hour, both in shared reading or writing and in the plenary. Research into classroom interactions by

Alexander (Carter 2003)[10] highlights the fact that interactions between teachers and children tend to be brief rather than sustained; closed questions predominate and children are very much focused on giving the right answer. There is little speculative talk and the 'child's answer marks the end of an exchange and the teacher's feedback formally closes it'. He recommends a move towards 'dialogic teaching' and identifies four conditions for effective dialogic teaching:

- *collective*: pupils and teachers address learning tasks together, whether as a group or as a class, rather than in isolation;
- *reciprocal*: pupils and teachers listen to each other, share ideas and consider alternative viewpoints;
- *cumulative*: pupils and teachers build on their own and each other's ideas and chain them into coherent lines of thinking and enquiry;
- *supportive*: pupils articulate their ideas freely, without fear of embarrassment over 'wrong' answers, and they help each other to reach common understandings.

In contrast, the community outside the classroom presents a rich and varied picture of language use, evolving language styles and of different communication practices. For many children whose mother tongue is not English, they are extremely adept at switching between two or more languages, depending on whom they are with. Although it is not always possible to replicate these practices in the classroom, teachers also need to take account of the children's linguistic repertoires outside of school and find ways to celebrate them in the classroom.

A climate for talk

A classroom ethos needs to be created where positive achievements in speaking and listening are valued and celebrated. The transitory and ephemeral nature of speech makes this difficult, but teachers can raise the profile of speaking and listening by making it the end product of an extended scheme of work (a debate which identifies arguments for and against a key question) or a role play which demonstrates children's understanding of a text they are reading. Talk can form the basis for discussion and analysis:

- Who do you feel most comfortable speaking and listening with?
- When do you feel most comfortable speaking and listening?
- Where do you feel most comfortable speaking and listening?
- What do you like discussing?
- Why?

Talk Diaries can raise the profile of speaking and listening for children. The first two hours of Rosie's (age 11) diary looked like this (Table 1.3).

Table 1.3 Talk Diary

TALK DIARY			
Who	**When**	**Where**	**Types of language**
Brother	Before school	At home	Questions – asking where clothes are. Responding to questions, 'Yes, I've done my homework.'
Friend/Mum	On the way to school	Mobile phone in the car	Asking friend to bring computer game to school. Listening to Mum. Arguing with brother.
Friends	Before school	Playground	Discussing. Arguing. Negotiating – how long can I have the game for? Organising – to meet at break-time.
Teacher	Beginning of school	Classroom	Answering my name.

A talk diary such as this also recognises children's speaking and listening outside of the classroom/school context and presents opportunities to discuss or contextualise language in its social context. Children, with the support of the teacher, can then begin to identify and discuss the kind of language they are using.

Good speakers and listeners

Children as young as 6 can provide thoughtful responses, demonstrating that they do in fact have a great deal of implicit understanding of the nature of talk and the role of the critical friend. The focus for this discussion was based on art.

'So what do you think makes a good speaker?'
   'My friend Aysha is a good speaker. When we're painting, she helps me. She says, "Why don't you use this colour here?" or "That bit's really good." It's nice to be told your work's good.'

Children should also be part of the process for valuing speaking and listening in the classroom: discussions of what makes a good speaker and a good listener can provide the basis for establishing shared and agreed ground rules for effective speaking and listening that can then be displayed on the classroom wall. This also serves to enhance and make explicit the place of speaking and listening in the classroom.

Different audiences

Providing different audiences is also a valuable way of raising the profile of speaking and listening – inviting other classes, teachers and parents to observe children engaged in a purposeful activity can fulfil a variety of functions, not least demonstrating that talk is a valued part of classroom practice. Both the media and Internet resources offer the opportunity to extend children's encounters with different speakers beyond the classroom. If children's reading of literature were confined to texts written by the class teacher or their peers, 'their knowledge of language would be unnecessarily limited';[11] the same must also be true of providing a limited number of role models for speaking and listening. Therefore, in providing both audiences and appropriate role models for spoken language, teachers need to exploit opportunities beyond the classroom.

Speaking and listening in the Literacy Hour

The National Curriculum for English (1999) stresses the interrelatedness of the four modes of language: speaking, listening, reading and writing. Research into effective practice in writing[12] also demonstrates that children make successful progress in their writing development when opportunities for speaking and listening are an integral part of work on reading and writing. Although teachers may feel there is immense pressure on time to fulfil the objectives from the Literacy Strategy in reading and writing alone, Goodwin states that: 'If anything, fulfilling the guidance of the framework requires more talk in the classroom rather than less' (2001: xi).

Whole-class teaching

Whole-class teaching provides the teacher with opportunities to model standard English in appropriate contexts and also to demonstrate the tentative and speculative nature of talk. Teachers' questions also play a key role in scaffolding children's learning, particularly in making progressively greater cognitive demands of the children through the use of higher order questions. When time is given for thought, reflection and support from talk partners, this context also provides a ready audience for children to give structured and extended contributions and to listen to and respond to the contributions made by other children in the classroom. Children's oral responses, moreover, provide opportunities for a teacher to assess a child's understanding and learning in a medium other than writing.

Group work

Children are used to sitting in groups as part of the organisational structure of the Literacy Hour. However, observational evidence shows that in general, children are working as individuals within those groups and not engaged in genuine collaboration on tasks which require exploratory talk. Teachers also need to consider carefully how they organise children for speaking and listening activities. Placing children in mixed ability groups can provide children with opportunities to interact with children who may be more linguistically competent. Gender is another significant consideration and, depending on the nature of the task, it may be appropriate to organise children into single sex groups. Children should also be given the opportunity for some autonomy on how groups are organised; this in itself can provide an interesting area for debate!

Drama activities can create the context for exploratory talk by encouraging the expression of hypothesis and opinion (Johnson 2001). In addition, children can be actively involved in making meaning from literary texts through the appropriate and selective use of DARTs (Directed Activities Related to Texts) activities.[13] These activities are not new; they were developed in the 1970s in response to research into reading which showed that children did a great deal of copying from texts, rather than actually gleaning information from their reading.

DARTS involves:

- cloze
- sequencing
- prediction.

Teachers frequently make use of the last strategy by stopping reading at a critical point in a narrative and asking children to predict or hypothesise what could happen next. Sequencing activities can work equally well with both fiction and non-fiction texts, requiring children to read and re-read parts of text in order to make meaning from the whole. Cloze activities provide interactive learning experiences where children can discuss, negotiate, speculate and justify word choices. In all DARTs activities, it is important to reassure children that they are not seeking the 'right' answer – but are searching for an appropriate answer.

The poem below provides an example of a text which is cognitively challenging but accessible to children of a range of abilities when presented in the right context. This involved Year 6 children as part of an extended scheme of work on Shakespeare. The work also encompassed History, where the children had been researching the life and times of Shakespeare and included a workshop from a theatre-in-education group which had focused on *A Midsummer Night's Dream*. In this context, children were becoming increasingly familiar with the rhythms and patterns of Shakespeare's language.

> My mistress' _____ are nothing like the sun;
> Coral is far more red than her lips red:
> If snow be white, why then her breasts are _____;
> If _____ be wires, black wires grow on her head.
> I have seen roses damask'd _____ and _____
> But no such roses see I in her cheeks:
> And in some perfumes is there more delight
> Than in the breath that from my mistress _____.
> I love to hear her _____, yet well I know
> That music hath a far more pleasing sound:
> I grant I never saw a goddess go –
> My _____ when she walks treads on the ground.
> And yet, by heaven, I think my love as rare
> As any she belied with false compare.[14]

(William Shakespeare)

The children worked together in pairs to negotiate and speculate about which words could fit into the spaces and then shared their ideas with larger groups (all mixed ability). The teacher commented on how much investigation (using dictionaries), counting (syllables) and discussion this activity provoked, not least in the arguments that ensued over the word 'reeks'. 'Shakespeare would never use that word. It's insulting and it's also too modern. Our word is better,' one group declared.

The plenary

The plenary offers time for opportunities for children's extended speaking and reflective listening. It also provides the teacher with the opportunity to assess children's understanding of texts through talk, as an alternative mode of assessment to writing. Children are often able to make positive, supportive comments about each other's work, but find it more difficult to be critical. By scaffolding their critical responses with language that articulates a speculative, considered approach, teachers can empower children to offer supportive criticism without being unduly challenging to their peers.

Some final thoughts

This chapter began by highlighting the fact that children know a great deal implicitly about talk and explored some ways in which teachers can seek to extend and develop this key area of language. In a recently overheard conversation which took place between a parent and her child after school, the mother enquired, 'What did your teacher say when you told her about your visit to London?' The five-year-old replied thoughtfully, 'She said, "Sit down and shut up, Andrew."' While it is possible to have sympathy for a beleaguered teacher in this context, it is also vital that children's voices are heard and valued in the classroom. The new guidance presents opportunities for schools and teachers to evaluate their own practice and place speaking and listening at the heart of the primary curriculum, not just in literacy teaching but in all subjects.

Notes

1. DfEE (1988).
2. Hines (2000). This novel tells the story of an adolescent boy, bullied both at home and at school, who finds solace in his relationship with a kestrel he has reared and trained.
3. Robin Alexander, writing in the *Education Weekly* of the *Guardian* on 19 April 2005.
4. The National Oracy Project was highly influential in informing the recommendations for the Speaking and Listening requirements of the English National Curriculum.
5. *Excellence and Enjoyment* was intended to give more autonomy back to schools so that schools themselves decided which aspects of a subject pupils would study in depth, how long to spend on each subject and how to arrange learning in the school day. It also identifies that one of the key ways to support literacy and numeracy is by reaffirming the place of speaking and listening both as a key foundation for literacy and as an essential aspect of all effective learning.
6. Unpublished research by Hodson based on data collected from 60 primary schools in West London. However, some LEAs, notably Barking and Dagenham and North Yorkshire, have launched major programmes focusing on classroom talk.
7. In the 1970s and 1980s, work done by Britton (1972) Halliday (1978) and Tizard and Hughes (1987) demonstrated that children play an active role in their language learning and are not merely imitating the language of adults. They build up a linguistic system (Halliday 1978) that is based on their current knowledge of language structures.
8. Vygotsky (1978).
9. QCA, 'Introducing the grammar of talk'. Research explored in *New Perspectives on Spoken English in the Classroom* (QCA 2003), speaking and listening requirements of the English National Curriculum.
10. Alexander, quoted by R. Carter in *New Perspectives on Spoken English in the Classroom* (QCA 2003).
11. Hewitt (2003).
12. Frater (2001).

13. Lunzer and Gardner (1979).
14. My mistress' eyes are nothing like the sun;
    Coral is far more red than her lips red:
    If snow be white, why then her breasts are dun;
    If hair be wires, black wires grow on her head.
    I have seen roses damask'd red and white
    But no such roses see I in her cheeks:
    And in some perfumes is there more delight
    Than in the breath that from my mistress reeks.
    I love to hear her speak, yet well I know
    That music hath a far more pleasing sound:
    I grant I never saw a goddess go –
    My mistress when she walks treads on the ground.
    And yet, by heaven, I think my love as rare
    As any she belied with false compare.

References and further reading

Britton, J. (1972) *Language and Learning*. London: Penguin.

DfEE (1998) *The National Literacy Strategy: Framework for Teaching*. London: HMSO.

DfEE (1999) *The National Curriculum: Handbook for Primary Teachers in England*. London: HMSO.

DfES (1988) *English for Ages 5–11*. London: HMSO.

DfES (2003a) *Excellence and Enjoyment: A Strategy for Primary Schools*. London: HMSO.

DfES (2003b) *Speaking, Listening, Learning: Working with Children in Key Stages 1 and 2*. London: HMSO.

Education Department of South Australia (2004a) *Oral Language Developmental Continuum*. Sydney: Rigby Heinemann.

Education Department of South Australia (2004b) *Oral Language Resource Book*. Sydney: Rigby Heinemann.

Fisher, R. and Williams, M. (eds) (2004) *Unlocking Creativity: Teaching Across the Curriculum*. London: David Fulton Publishers.

Frater, G. (2001) *Effective Practice in Writing at KS2*. London: Basic Skills Agency.

Goodwin, P. (ed.) (2001) *The Articulate Classroom*. London: David Fulton Publishers.

Grugeon, E., Dawes, L., Smith, C. and Hubbard, L. (eds) (2005) *Teaching Speaking and Listening in the Primary School*. London: David Fulton Publishers.

Halliday, M.A.K. (1978) *Language as Social Semiotic*. London: Edward Arnold.

Hewitt, R. (2003) 'Is there a case for considering talk as part of the oral heritage and as a performance skill?', in QCA *New Perspectives on Spoken English in the Classroom*. Suffolk: QCA.

Hines, B. (2000) *A Kestrel for a Knave*. Harmondsworth: Penguin.

Johnson, C. (2001), in Fisher, R. and Williams, M. *Unlocking Literacy: A Guide for Teachers*. London: David Fulton Publishers.

Lunzer, E. and Gardner, K. (1979) *The Effective Use of Reading*. London: Heinemann.

QCA (2003) *New Perspectives on Spoken English in the Classroom*. Suffolk: QCA.

Tizard, B. and Hughes, M. (1987) 'The intellectual search of young children', in Pollard, A. *Children and Their Primary Schools*. London: Falmer Press.

Vygotsky, L.S. (1978) *Mind in Society: The Development of Higher Psychological Processes*. Cambridge. MA: Harvard University Press.

Fostering speaking and listening in Foundation Stage classrooms

Hilma Rask

The aim of this chapter is to explore the role of speaking and listening in developing and extending children's learning in the Foundation Stage of education. The importance of the teacher as both an active listener and an expert companion in dialogue with children will be discussed. It will be argued that teachers gain insights into children's learning when they reflect upon what young children actually say and do during their play activities. Finally, it will be emphasised that in the light of such reflection, teachers learn to take appropriate action to further enrich language learning provision for the children in their care. Throughout the chapter, vignettes from classroom observations will be used to illustrate ways in which purposeful speaking and listening can foster children's learning in early years settings. Effective strategies for developing and extending young children's speaking and listening skills will also be discussed.

A rationale for speaking and listening

One of the most important contributions to understanding how children learn has been proposed through Vygotsky's (1978) model of the 'zone of proximal development'. His research suggested that learning takes place most effectively within a context of social interaction through the joint construction of meaning.[1] With the help of a more competent adult or peer, a child is able to move towards new learning (Vygotsky 1978). This idea also influenced the research of Jerome Bruner (1986) with his proposal that the more experienced adult or peer acts as a 'scaffold' for new learning. Vygotsky emphasised the vital linkages between thought and language. Bruner also aptly described language as 'a tool of thought'. What is important for the teacher in the light of this research, is to consider the key role of the adult in providing the necessary scaffolds for learning in the classroom which extend children's knowledge, skills and understanding through talk and action. What the child can do in co-operation with a more experienced learner, such as the teacher, enables the child to move towards new learning. Clearly, speaking and listening has a vital role in the process of learning.

In his longitudinal Bristol-based study, Wells (1986) documented the often complex dialogues which took place between children and their mother because there were known shared contexts and reference points in their own familiar world. His research also indicated that listening to, reading and talking about stories together at home in the early years of life brought significant benefits for future literacy learning at school. Such experiences challenged children towards an understanding of language out of direct context, for they learned to make meaning from words alone.[2] This is important research with implications for teachers of young children.

What an extraordinary feat young children achieve within the first six years of their lives. By the age of 6 a child's language is in many instances close to that of an adult speaker (de Villiers and de Villiers 1979). By this time, the majority of young children have grasped many of the rules that govern the structure of the particular spoken language to which they have been exposed.[3] Indeed, many children have grasped the structural patterns and vocabulary of additional languages within the home as well. The teacher of young children has a vital role to play in supporting the continuing development of language skills and competences, alongside parents, carers and peers.

In order to become a fluent communicator, the young child has to learn the sound system within that language, that is, the phonology. They need to grasp ways in which language is fitted together and structured: the syntax. In addition, they need to understand the semantics of the language, which is the meaning of it all. Finally, they need to understand the ways in which language is used in particular contexts and settings, known as the pragmatics of language. Language is not only social. It is a way of sharing meaning between people, and it is a means of learning and cognition.

High quality teaching of speaking and listening has a direct impact on children's learning and their standards of achievement (DfES 2003).[4] Throughout their schooling pupils gain from being able to articulate their ideas with clarity and from the ability to listen with accuracy and with increasingly critical analysis. Through collaboration and group discussions, pupils learn to take account of the views of others and to listen with attention and accuracy. They learn to take turns, negotiate and to modify their views on a particular issue in the light of other spoken contributions. Drama also has an important place in the development of oral confidence and early literacy (Hendy 1996),[5] since this enables pupils to take on the roles of other characters, express feelings and explore issues (DfEE 1999). The seedbed of all these aspects is in the early years setting. Helping young children to develop accurate listening skills is an important aspect of their early learning and is likely to impact on their future literacy learning. It is important that the early speaking and listening skills which are fostered in the Foundation Stage of education have continuing focus and status across the curriculum areas during the next stages of education (DfES 2003).

Listening to children talking: assessing speaking and listening skills

The guidance provided for the Foundation Stage curriculum offers the teacher a valuable framework of progression through the use of the stepping stones[6] which set out the development of listening and speaking skills (DfEE 2000). This provides the teacher with the broad brush strokes within which both to plan for individual needs, and to monitor development along the continuum of language learning. Also useful are the guidelines issued on the progression of speaking and listening skills for pupils new to learning English, as these provide additional guidance to be used in conjunction with the stepping stones when planning for the needs of bilingual pupils and assessing their progress over time (QCA 2000).

Effective assessment needs to be continual, curricular, consultative and communicative (Jones 2002). The universal introduction of Foundation Stage profiling across schools in England and Wales provides schools with useful additional data for use in tracking and monitoring children's progress throughout their time in school. When routine and systematic record-keeping procedures become embedded within the classroom, a valuable cumulative record of progress emerges over time. Many teachers have found it useful to make use of Post-it® notes or self-adhesive label rolls which can be easily attached to a larger record sheet, as they recognise the need to seize the moment, to note down what children do and say during their play and activities. This helps in the cycle of planning, providing insights into children's learning processes and current levels of linguistic knowledge and understanding, which informs future planning (DfEE 2000).[7] For example, the teacher might discover that a child needs more experience of the same activity to consolidate learning. She may need a new range of activities to further embed conceptual language learning, or she may need new challenges in another direction, having demonstrated full conceptual understanding through her talk and actions.

Schools able to establish close links with local feeder playgroups and nursery providers know the value of such partnerships, where mutual exchange visits enable staff to further observe and discuss children's language and learning prior to and after the transition to school. It is important that assessment procedures acknowledge parental contributions and that information is comprehensively shared with parents and carers. Young children themselves can be capable contributors to their own assessments. This is an area where more research could be directed in the future. There are clear indicators that young children are able to do more than they are often invited to. For example, when making visual representations of children's block play for their own analysis, the researchers reported how the children sought to involve themselves in this activity as well and were keen to talk about their plans (Gura 1992).[8]

Teachers talking and listening

Listening is not the same as hearing. The listening teacher has to attend to what the child actually does and says in particular contexts and interpret the underlying meaning of utterances. For example, a child's spoken response may reveal how well he understands a task or a new concept. It may reveal the exact nature of any misapprehensions. There is another aspect of listening too, which is to recognise, from the tone of voice for example, when a child is asking for help. A child may reach a level of frustration or despondency where adult support or intervention may be needed.

In a session which I undertook with trainee teachers a few years ago, the students were asked to work in pairs and to listen to each other's account of a discipline incident encountered during a recent school experience placement. Individuals were later asked to recall their partner's account. A significant number of students were shocked to discover that they found it difficult to recall their partner's account with accuracy. One student mentioned that she had been so busy rehearsing her own story in her head that she had not fully attended to the speaker. This exercise considerably heightened student awareness of listening with attention.

It is helpful to consider the differences in verbal response which might be brought about by the use of closed questions, such as 'what?' and 'where?', as opposed to the more open-ended 'why?' and 'how might?' Certainly the latter types of questions are more likely to encourage greater reflection and hypothesis. In an insightful article, Cousins (1990)[9] relates how Sonnyboy, a five-year-old traveller child in a reception class, was puzzled, and no doubt irritated, by the teacher asking questions to which it was clear that she already knew the answer!

The next section will draw upon examples from the classroom, presented as illustrative vignettes which investigate aspects of speaking and listening in a range of early years settings.

Celebrations of speaking and listening in the early years: reflections on practice

Circle discussion in the nursery

> Gail, the teacher in charge of a multilingual nursery class, has asked the children to sit in a circle and joins them for a short discussion of their activities. Dennis, the child on her right, says, 'I am next to you.' Baljit, the child on her left, responds with, 'And I am next to you too.' Gail smiles to them both and says, 'Yes, you are both next to me, and I am in the middle.' They all laugh and nod in agreement.

At first glance this kind of talk sounds very ordinary, hardly worthy of inclusion as illustrative material. What is so special about this dialogue? Simply because it is the kind of talk which good teachers engage in constantly in early years settings. Gail automatically and systematically acts as the experienced other, that more experienced talker and listener, who can scaffold new learning (Bruner 1986). She takes her conversational cues from the language offered by the children and she adds on new elements to extend and expand linguistic and conceptual usage. Here, for example, she adds on the prepositional phrase 'in the middle', while acknowledging and valuing the children's use of the preposition 'next to'. She does this in a context which makes the meaning totally explicit, for Gail is an artful opportunist in guiding and extending children's talk through routine daily activities in the classroom. When Gail orchestrates activities in her busy multilingual nursery, she is constantly alert to what children say and do. Sometimes she rephrases the talk which children offer, in order to clarify and to make their meaning clear to others. She extends and elaborates through the use of her own carefully chosen vocabulary. Her use of the structural patterns of English is always appropriate to the needs of individuals and their current level of oral competence. She exploits real concrete experiences to make meaning clear and to establish exactly what the children know and understand (Nutbrown 1996).[10] When Gail asks questions of her young audience, they are rarely of a closed nature where the answer is either right or wrong. Instead, she opens up enquiry, invites speculation and early hypothesis through the use of genuine open-ended questions. For example, she asks two boys constructing a tall tower outdoors, 'I wonder what will happen if you add one more brick?' To a group of children who have discovered ants in the sand tray, she asks, 'Why do you think the ants got into our sand tray?' and she listens with genuine interest to their somewhat unusual ideas. In such ways she provides rich early experiences of speaking and listening, in the context of purposeful planned learning activities (DfEE 2000).

The great big giant: drama and talk

Two small boys greeted the visitor at the door, excitedly calling out, 'Come on, come and see our giant. He's so big.'

'Yeah, we've got a giant over there, and he's friendly and all.'

The giant had moved in over the weekend. In his long stripy sweater and elephant-sized trousers, he draped amiably over the tented storytelling and book area in the reception classroom. His arrival had provoked intense excitement, and the student teacher encouraged speculation through questions such as 'I wonder where he came from?' She asked what kind of books a giant might like to read, and invited the children to find some in their class book collection, which she had supplemented in advance. The children began to ask their own questions such as where the giant would sleep in the classroom at night. They were encouraged to suggest ways in which to make the giant feel welcome and happy.

The giant proved to be a real charmer at encouraging a great variety of talk, although he never actually spoke directly, only through reported speech and alleged whispers. Encouraged by his reassuring bulk and seemingly endless patience, children turned the pages of selected 'giant story books' for him and made up giant stories for his entertainment. Occasionally, one particular child, with a troubled home life, would cuddle up to this tireless listener for a quiet chat.

This example illustrates the power of dramatic events such as the introduction of a large puppet, or an imaginary person visiting a classroom for a period of time as an additional stimulus for focused talk. For young children such events can provide a link between their imaginative play and the world of children's literature. Speaking and listening skills can be greatly enhanced and exploited through the provision of vivid visual and concrete experiences, and this can provide an additional gateway through to emerging literacy skills (DfEE 2000).

Further suggestions might include:

- a visit from a familiar folk tale character, such as Little Red Riding Hood, Goldilocks or one of the three bears;
- puppet toys and a simple puppet theatre to hide behind for anonymity;
- a mystery bag found in the classroom full of, for example, food items from the story of the very hungry caterpillar (Carle 1970);

- various items such as objects from a well-known story, strategically hidden around the classroom;
- the teacher appearing dressed in the role of a story character, ready to answer questions from the children about the story;
- large masks for children to re-enact a favourite story together in a role play area set aside in the room;
- the construction of simple buildings for role play purposes such as a large castle or pirate ship, or vet's surgery.

Making soup: promoting discussion through practical tasks

It was the tantalising smell that enticed me into the classroom. It was a wholesome, Grandma's kitchen aroma of good things to eat. Aah! It was vegetable soup. The children in the reception class had worked in small groups, cutting, tasting and talking together with adult helpers about the taste, texture, feel, shape, colour of a range of different vegetables. Some of the vegetables were unfamiliar to different children and it had been a chance to share diverse knowledge from their home lives, through well-planned adult-led discussions. They had taken their large pot of soup to the kitchen where cook had kindly put it on her cooker to heat. The soup had been returned later and now the children were ready to taste it.'

Teacher: *Ooh, mine's delicious. It's lovely and hot and I can taste lots of the different vegetables that we put in. They don't taste crunchy now, do they?*

David: *No, they are kind of squishy. Ooh, mine's lovely and hot too! It's yummy!*

Kylie: *So is mine. It's kind of chunky. Mine is kind of chunky. Look! (holding out a spoonful)*

Yasar: *Mmm. I got a carrot, kind of chunky, look!*

Dean: *Ugh! Yuk! Mine is all lumpy, but I like the sweetcorn bits.*

Teacher: *Do you eat soup at home, Dean?*

Dean: *No! I hate soup! (vehemently) But I like our soup, 'cos we made it and it's lovely.*

The teacher and teaching assistant worked in a well-co-ordinated team, and had invited parent helpers to join in the morning's activity. Before the session took place they had all talked together briefly about the purposes of the activities and the teacher had listed the key vocabulary and the kinds of questions that she would like the adults to discuss with children during the preparation of the vegetable soup, to explore taste and texture. In this way, the teacher and her colleagues were able to introduce new vocabulary to the children and encourage the articulation of thoughts and feelings relating to the activity. It is useful to note how Yasar, a bilingual child not yet fully fluent in English, benefited from the group talk. He learned to use the phrase 'kind of chunky' which was modelled by another child, because the talk was embedded in a meaningful practical context which supported his understanding appropriately, alongside his peers.[11]

Making houses: observation and intervention in the role play area

The final-year student in the reception class was being observed by a senior colleague who was acting as her mentor. They had formed a good relationship of trust and mutual respect (TTA 2001).[12] The focus of the activities was based on the story of the three little pigs. The student teacher worked with a group of six children making books about the story, after a highly stimulating whole-class exploration of the text. She had asked her teaching assistant to support a second group of less experienced writers with a simpler sequencing task. The rest of the class were to be engaged in self-chosen activities relating to the story which had been set up in the adjoining area.

The free choice activities had been carefully set up. The children had been challenged to construct different houses for the three little pigs using large sticks, bundles of straw and construction bricks. The children started the tasks with enthusiasm, but it was evident that as soon as they came up against a challenge which they were unable to resolve, they moved away from the activity and moved to a different task. Very soon the majority of children had moved to the nearby sand tray. Their play was becoming repetitive and much of the talk was now social chatter. The observer noticed that one boy stayed at the sticks for a sustained period of time and attempted to place the sticks together. He said aloud, to nobody in particular, 'This one is too short. It won't fit.' After several attempts, he gave up and walked off.

The mentor, the classroom assistant and the student had a very useful discussion of the lesson and evaluated together what had gone really well, such as the whole-class story focus, and then discussed what could be improved. They decided that the construction tasks required more adult intervention through talk and observation, if the intended conceptual language learning was to take place. They identified that the problem was an organisational and management issue. The student decided to deploy the classroom assistant to work with children in the construction activities and see what happened to the children's talk and learning as a result of this. She would continue to work with a group on the book-making discussion task and would additionally manage the work of the second group undertaking the sequencing task. She arranged to change roles with her colleague half-way through the session, in order to monitor all the learning.

The next day there was a noticeable change in both the children's interest and engagement with the construction tasks and the quality of their talk as they worked alongside an interested adult. The skilled teaching assistant discussed the problem of joining the sticks together with the children and drew their attention to the range of joining materials such as raffia, string, masking tape and glue that had been provided. The children talked animatedly to her about their discoveries, as they tried out different ways of joining sticks and the straw bundles to make houses. Of particular note was the way in which most individuals began to use the conceptual mathematical vocabulary introduced and reinforced by the teaching assistant, such as 'much too short', 'not thick enough' and 'too long'. As arranged, the student teacher and the teaching assistant changed roles and the student continued the discussion with the children during the construction tasks. She noticed, for example, that a normally rather reserved girl offered complex sentences when she excitedly explained how she selected sticks of exactly the same length to use. This child revealed much greater knowledge and understanding of the process than had been anticipated.

Talking about the session afterwards, both adults considered that this had been an invaluable opportunity to reflect on their approaches and decided to continue with this pattern of working. The student teacher commented that it was easy to think that the children would learn just because the play activities were well set up and inviting. 'But unless you actually listen to what they are saying and talk with them about it all, you don't really know what they have been learning and what they need to learn next. The trouble is you can't be everywhere at once, so you have to use your time really well.'

This example highlights the value of reflection on practice (TTA 2001).[13] It illustrates how the student teacher was able to considerably improve the provision she had made for language and learning through reviewing the management and organisation of her planned curriculum. It also offers an insight into the valuable professional dialogue which can emerge within the mentoring process.

Paired discussion after a story

The storytelling session in the reception class was utterly spellbinding. Silence reigned, as for the first time, Geoff, the student teacher, read the story *We're Going on a Bear Hunt* (Rosen 1989) from an enlarged text, which all on the carpet area could see. He employed the full range of his voice to develop the dramatic features of the written story. The children's faces were full of wonder and delight as they listened to the unfolding story. After that first reading, there were invitations for the whole class to join in with the fun-filled alliterative phrases and actions which made up the story events. Later the children worked in partners, sitting face to face, saying the repeated phrases together when the teacher paused appropriately in his reading of the text. Later in the week the children worked in their partner pairs again. This time they were challenged to recall, unaided, the whole sequence of the story line. Geoff and his assistant moved around the carpet area to listen for accuracy, and to offer support where needed.

Paired work can be exploited well during whole-class sessions. This arrangement provides a useful strategy for ensuring that everyone has the maximum chance to talk. It also encourages more hesitant children to participate because they address an audience of one rather than the whole group, and because other pairs are busy talking at the same time. Some teachers find it effective to pre-select pairs, for example, pairing a very articulate child with a less confident partner, or a bilingual child not yet fully fluent in English. Others prefer to make pairs based on friendship or on a random basis which changes regularly. Children receiving additional learning or behaviour support from a teaching assistant often gain from working with this adult partner at such times. Through the use of additional pictorial material or gestures this adult can provide further contextual cues which aid recall, oral confidence and understanding.

A spaceship in the nursery: exploring role play and emergent literacy talk

It was the biggest cardboard box that Sasha, the nursery student teacher, had been able to find and out of it she created a colourful but rudimentary spaceship for her nursery class. She had thought long and hard about what she wanted to provide in this context to encourage both imaginative role play and early literacy behaviour. After an introductory time when, wearing helmets and white overalls, children were encouraged to take on the roles of space astronauts, Sasha had introduced a range of different writing and recording materials into the spaceship. For example, there were squared grids on clipboards, with pencils attached on string, notepads, an old computer keyboard, Post-it® notes and recycled diaries and calendars. Over the next few weeks, Sasha noticed that not only were the children starting to participate in new ways as emergent writers, but also their talk started to reflect their growing understanding of the purposes of recording both numerals and language. For example, one child directed his co-pilot to record the number of stars they had 'seen', using the grid board. Sasha made sure that she talked about their recorded material during and after their play, and this showed the children that their discoveries and recordings had status, and were listened to by an enthusiastic audience. Talking helped the children to recall their ideas even though the mark making was of a very simple form for the youngest and less experienced children.

This illustration highlights the importance of providing both for imaginative role play to encourage speaking and listening skills development and for the nurturing of early literacy talk. It is a clear example of how a carefully structured early years curriculum provides for effective learning (DfEE 2000). In this instance, the student teacher provided good opportunities for children to communicate their thoughts, feelings and ideas through taking on the roles of space explorers in their play. An added dimension was provided by the well-planned provision of writing and recording materials which promoted early literacy talk and experiences in a purposeful context. Activities such as this are known to provide valuable insights for children into the links between speech and writing.[14]

Playing with language: developing phonological awareness in the nursery through games, songs and rhymes.

Penny, a nursery teacher in charge of a large inner-city multilingual nursery, ensures that she provides time during the day for the children to build up a repertoire of familiar songs, nursery rhymes and jingles. The children respond to these routine shared times with increasing delight and are eager participants. Penny has noticed the particular benefits which bilingual children who are at a very early stage of learning English gain from these sessions. The more confident of these children join in with repeated chorus lines and phrases, while less confident children sometimes join in with actions and gestures. They also listen with increasing attention, especially when Penny uses additional visual aids for counting verses such as, 'five currant buns from the baker's shop'.

Penny is alert to the need to keep the sessions short, sharply focused and, above all, motivating and fun-filled. She uses a great variety of simple games to encourage the children to play with the sounds of the English language. For example, the children walk through puddles saying, 'Splish, splash, splosh. I need a wash.' They shake imaginary jellies saying, 'Wibble wobble, wibble wobble, jelly on a plate!' Penny has noticed that many children spontaneously try out their own rhyming sounds as they play together. It seems clear to her that children are experimenting with the sounds of language and that they find this to be great fun. For example, Penny noticed that two boys playing at the water tray were in endless giggles as over and over again, they repeated the phrase, 'Silly Billy', which they had heard from a parent helper.

Penny takes time to listen to individual responses during shared song and rhyme sessions, sometimes directing her nursery nurse colleague to lead the session while she notes and attends to individual responses and participation. This enables her to identify children who may be slow to respond, or do not listen with accuracy. These are children she identifies for additional small-group focus.

Penny has also run a parent workshop where she included a session on the use of familiar nursery rhymes, songs and jingles and made available a selection of tapes and games for home use. Several parents have mentioned that they are enjoying sharing these activities at home and that older and younger siblings have also joined in, as well as some grandparents.

Penny is aware of the value of developing early phonological awareness through the medium of language games, songs and rhymes. She knows that research evidence suggests a close correlation between good pre-school phonological knowledge and understanding and later success in reading, even taking account of different intelligence levels and social backgrounds of the children (Bradley and Bryant 1983). She has taken good account in her own practice of the research which identifies early sensitivity to onset and rime as a vital factor for later success in reading and writing, and she is aware that learning nursery rhymes benefits future literacy (Goswami and Bryant 1990, Maclean *et al.* 1993).[15] Penny takes every opportunity to provide the children in her care with time to play with language through activities which they enjoy and which develop early phonological skills. Penny also actively encourages parents to spend time at home sharing nursery rhymes and jingles. This leads the children to experiment and reflect upon language together with their teacher and other significant adults.

Some final reflections on speaking and listening in the classroom

While undertaking a small-scale research project which focused on factors that enable young able children to develop and extend their literacy, one of the significant features which emerged was the children's ability to talk coherently about their own learning strategies (Williams and Rask 2000).[16] This is known as metacognition (Fisher 1998).[17] For example, 6-year-old Mark explained how he had read the unusual word 'scythe'. He confided, 'At first I thought it said "sky".' He mentioned that the picture cue had been of no use, 'because it looked like a pickaxe'. He went on to explain that he recalled the word from last week's comic. He said, 'Yes, they put scythes on the dummies so that the foreman thought it was them at work, 'cos he was the most short-sighted man in comic land.' He demonstrated through his talk that he had understood the text. He also revealed that he knew a good range of the cue systems through which to gain meaning from written texts. Approaches in the classroom which facilitate plenty of well-focused small-group discussions between teachers and children provide rich opportunities to engage in dialogues. Such discussions offer deeper insights into thinking and learning processes, for all concerned.

Early on in my own career as a young teacher, I learned an important lesson relating to speaking and listening and the power of words. It raised a wry smile among a student teacher audience whenever I shared it with them, and hopefully encouraged students to reflect carefully upon the messages their own words would give to the children they were about to teach.

Maria plays at school: a lesson for her teacher

I looked around my multilingual classroom, taking what I had come to call my talking health check. This consisted of a short tracking observation of activities of targeted children. I noted the four children at the listening station, earphones on, animatedly joining in with the folk tale story of the Gingerbread Man as they followed the text in their own booklets. I noted the three girls seated together on a rug, retelling the same story together, using the figurines on a magnet board. Things were going well, I thought to myself. This is a classroom where talking and listening is valued.

It was then I noticed her. Four-year-old Maria, a Spanish mother tongue speaker, alone in the home corner. She appeared to be speaking in English, although her preferred language when playing alone was Spanish. I could not wait to hear what she was saying. I crept closer. Maria sat on a chair, clutching a capacious handbag. She was surrounded by an orderly array of assorted dolls and toy animals on a small rug. To my eternal shame, I heard her say, in the parrot perfect voice of her teacher, 'Sit down children! I said, be quiet! Be quiet!' Maria was playing at schools.

Maria's message was a profound one. Over the years it has served to remind me of the need for continual critical reflection on what we espouse as educators and what we actually do and say as practitioners each day. Her message emphasises that children's voices can both inform the teacher, and direct future planning for teaching and learning. If I could hear Maria now, I hope she would be saying these words, instead: 'Keep talking children. I am listening. I am attending.'

Notes

1. A useful discussion on the contributions of Vygotsky and Bruner to understanding the language and learning process is offered in Sutherland (1992).
2. Although the focus of this study involved a sample of mothers talking with their children, the evidence base was wide and the findings of much significance. See Wells (1986).
3. An absorbing and thought-provoking source on language acquisition is found in Crystal (1987).
4. Although addressed to teachers of pupils in Key Stages 1 and 2. This booklet is essential reading for Foundation Stage teachers, as it provides linkages with the next stage of learning, see DfES (2003).
5. Useful ideas for exploiting drama and story making are presented in Hendy (1996).
6. Teachers find it useful to plan directly from the stepping stones level charts when planning for the full range of language and learning needs of the children, see DfEE (2000).
7. DfEE (2000) sets out a clear set of principles to guide practice and emphasises that children learn in different ways and at different rates.
8. An excellent account of research directed by Tina Bruce and the Froebel Blockplay Research Group which explores children talking and learning together, is provided in Gura (1992).
9. Cousins (1990) '"Are your little Humpty Dumpties sinking or floating?" What sense do young children of four make of the reception class at a school? Different conceptions at time of transition'. In this fascinating article, Sonnyboy, a Traveller child, is heard to ask why the teacher keeps asking what colour things are, for it is patently obvious to him that she must know the answers to her own question.
10. Nutbrown argues a cogent case for respectful observations of children at play in Nutbrown (1996).
11. Gravelle (1996) offers a particularly comprehensive rationale for effective ways in which to support bilingual pupils in school.
12. The booklet published by the TTA (2001) *The Role of the Induction Tutor: Principles and Guidance* gives examples of how such mentoring roles can be constructively continued for NQTs during their induction year and beyond.
13. The value of reflective practice is highlighted in the above publication (TTA 2001) when mentors and newly qualified teachers discuss how factual feedback statements and open-ended questioning encourages reflection.
14. Browne (1993) offers many practical examples of how teachers can make the necessary links between spoken language and the development of early writing skills.

15. Research undertaken by Maclean, Bryant and Bradley (1987) found very strong connections between awareness of rhyme and knowledge of nursery rhymes, and how this has a positive impact on later literacy success.
16. Williams and Rask (2000). Fuller exploration of able young children, school and family factors is included in this article.
17. Metacognition, the ability to reflect upon one's own learning processes, is discussed in more detail in Fisher (1998).

References and further reading

Bradley, L. and Bryant, P.E. (1983) 'Categorising sounds and learning to read: a causal connection', *Nature*, 310: 419–21.

Browne, A. (1993) *Helping Children to Write*. London: Paul Chapman Publishing.

Bruner, J. (1986) *Actual Minds, Possible Worlds*. Cambridge, MA: Harvard University Press.

Carle, E. (1970) *The Very Hungry Caterpillar*. London: Hamish Hamilton.

Cousins, J. (1990) '"Are your little Humpty Dumpties sinking or floating?" What sense do children of four make of the reception class at school? Different conceptions at the time of transition', *Early Years*, 10(2): 28–31.

Crystal, D. (1987) *The Cambridge Encyclopaedia of Language*. Cambridge: Cambridge University Press.

de Villiers, P. and de Villiers, J. (1979) *Early Language*. Glasgow: Collins.

DfEE (1999) *Opportunities for Drama in the Framework of Objectives*. London; HMSO.

DfEE (2000) *Curriculum Guidance for the Foundation Stage*. London: QCA.

DfES (2001a) *Children with English as an Additional Language in the National Literacy Strategy: Framework for Teaching*. London: HMSO.

DfES (2001b) *Code of Practice for Pupils with Special Educational Needs*. London: QCA.

DfES (2003) *Speaking, Listening, Learning: Working with Children in Key Stages 1 and 2*. London: QCA.

Fisher, R. (1998) 'Thinking about thinking: developing metacognition in children, *Early Child Development and Care*, 141: 1–13.

Goswami, U. and Bryant, P. (1990) *Phonological Skills and Learning to Read*. Hove: Lawrence Erlbaum Associates.

Gravelle, M. (1996) *Supporting Bilingual Learners in Schools*. Stoke-on-Trent: Trentham Books.

Gravelle, M. (ed.) (2000) *Planning for Bilingual Learners: An Inclusive Curriculum*. Stoke-on-Trent: Trentham Books.

Gura, P. (1992) *Exploring Learning: Young Children and Block Play*. London: Paul Chapman Publishing.

Hendy, L. (1996) 'It is only a story, isn't it? Drama in the form of interactive story making in the early years classroom', in D. Whitebread (ed.) *Teaching and Learning in the Early Years*. London: Routledge.

Jones, D. (2002) 'Keeping track: assessment in writing', in M. Williams (ed.) *Unlocking Writing*. London: David Fulton Publishers.

Maclean, M., Bryant, P. and Bradley, L. (1987) 'Rhymes, nursery rhymes and reading in early childhood', *Merrill Palmer Quarterly*, 33(3): 255–81.

Nutbrown, C. (ed.) (1996) *Respectful Educators, Capable Learners: Children's Rights and Early Education*. London: Paul Chapman Publishing.

QCA (1999) *Target Setting and Assessment in the National Literacy Strategy.* London: QCA.

QCA (2000) *A Language in Common: Assessing English as an Additional Language.* London: QCA.

Rosen, M. (1989) *We're Going on a Bear Hunt.* London: Walker Books.

Sutherland, P. (1992) *Cognitive Development Today: Piaget and His Critics.* London: Paul Chapman Publishing.

TTA (2001) *The Role of the Induction Tutor: Principles and Guidance.* London: TTA.

Vygotsky, L.S. (1978) *Mind in Society: The Development of Higher Psychological Processes.* Cambridge, MA: Harvard University Press.

Wells, G. (1986) *The Meaning Makers: Children Learning Language and Using Language to Learn.* London: Hodder and Stoughton.

Whitebread, D. (ed.) (1996) *Teaching and Learning in the Early Years.* London: Routledge.

Williams, M. and Rask, H. (2000) 'The identification of variables which enable able children in year one to extend and develop their literacy skills'. *Gifted and Talented*, 4(2), November.

Wood, D. (1988) *How Children Think and Learn.* Oxford: Basil Blackwell.

Talking to think: why children need philosophical discussion

Robert Fisher

Thinking has to be learned in the way dancing has to be learned.

(Nietzsche 1888)

Philosophy is good because it gets you to use parts of the brain you don't use in other lessons.

(Karl, age 10)

'Why is speaking and listening important?' I asked a group of nine-year-olds. 'It helps to think,' said Andrea. 'It helps to build your brain,' said Dan. 'You learn more,' said Pat. They were surely right. Human intelligence is primarily developed through speaking and listening. The quality of our lives depends on the quality of our thinking and on our ability to communicate and discuss what we think with others. Talk is intrinsic to literacy and to our ability to form relationships with others. It is the foundation of both IQ (verbal intelligence) and EQ (emotional intelligence). Every lesson therefore should include some time for 'talking to think'.

This chapter is about a special form of 'talking to think' based on an approach called 'Philosophy for Children' (P4C).[1] It is a form of dialogic teaching that emphasises the development of critical and creative thinking through questioning and dialogue between children and teachers and between children and children. Researchers have reported striking cognitive gains through this approach in the classroom.[2] Philosophy for Children can help enhance communicative skills as well as develop habits of intelligent behaviour. These habits of intelligent behaviour include being:

- *curious:* through asking deep and interesting questions;
- *collaborative:* through engaging in thoughtful discussion;
- *critical:* through giving reasons and evidence;

- creative: through generating and building on ideas;
- caring: through developing awareness of self and care of others.

Philosophical discussion develops the kinds of thinking, as Karl says, that children may not use in other lessons, including *philosophical intelligence* – the capacity to ask and seek answers to existential questions. Second, philosophical enquiry provides a means for children to develop *discussion skills* – the capacity to engage in thoughtful conversations with others. Third, philosophical discussion of complex objects of intellectual enquiry, such as stories, enhances *critical thinking* and verbal reasoning – the capacity to draw inferences and deductions from all kinds of texts. Fourth, philosophical enquiry helps develop *creative thinking* – the capacity to generate hypotheses and build on the ideas of others. Fifth, doing philosophy with children helps develop *emotional intelligence* – the capacity to be self-aware and caring towards others, providing essential practice in *active citizenship* and participative democracy. The chapter concludes with a warning about the challenges that can arise from engaging in talk for thinking.

Being curious: asking open questions

Studies of interaction in the classroom in the past 50 years have consistently shown that it is teacher-talk that dominates the classroom and that in much of this talk there is a lack of open questioning.[3] Such studies show that often in teacher-led discussions closed questions predominate, children only make brief responses, teacher–talk rarely challenged children's thinking and that pupil-pupil discussion (rather than gossip) was rare.

An open question is one that allows for a range of possible answers. A closed question allows for only a true or false answer. One of the problems that results from teachers using too many closed questions is that it leads over the years to a decline in the curiosity of children. The need to test and 'cover' the curriculum leads to students asking fewer questions the older they get.[4]

Open questions, like those used by Socrates in ancient Greece, have many potential benefits. Like closed questions, they can offer cognitive challenge, but they also do the following:

- encourage more flexible thinking;
- allow depth of discussion;
- test the limits of knowledge rather than one item of knowledge;
- encourage better assessment of children's beliefs;
- offer the possibility to clear up misunderstandings;

- result in unanticipated and unexpected answers, new hypotheses and connections to previous knowledge.

A 10-year-old child who was asked in a P4C session 'Is there a difference between knowing something and believing something?' replied, 'Yes, there is, because, for example, I believe in Father Christmas, but I know he doesn't exist!'

Teaching for thinking requires a community approach to enquiry in the classroom, not one or two voices creating single viewpoints, but many voices creating multiple viewpoints. The community of enquiry is sustained by the use of complex open-ended questions and elaborate explanatory responses – by teachers as well as children. For example, a teacher using a story that includes the theme of truth (such as Aesop's fable 'Mercury and the Axe') might prepare a number of open-ended prompt questions to encourage children to discuss the nature of truth. The following is a list of such questions that have been used in many primary classes.[5]

Thinking about telling the truth

Key question: What is truth?

1　Do you think this is a true story? Why?
2　What do we mean when we say something is true?
3　What do we call something that is not true? What does 'false' mean?
4　What is a lie?
5　What do we call a story which is not true? What is fiction/a fable/a fairy tale?
6　Which character in the story was honest? What does 'honest' mean?
7　Which character in the story was a liar? What does 'liar' mean?
8　Is it better to tell the truth or lies? Why?
9　Have you ever told a lie? Can you say when or why?
10　Is it ever right to tell a lie? Is it ever wrong to tell the truth?

Here is an excerpt from one such classroom discussion, prompted by the teacher using questions like those above:

Child 1:　*Sometimes you say something you think is true. It's not a lie if you think it is true.*

Child 2:　*I disagree with that because you could think something was true and say it was true when it was not true.*

Teacher:　*Can you give an example?*

Child 2:   *Well, if you could say it is raining because you thought it was raining and it was only birds on the roof. You can say something you think is true although in fact it is not true.*

Child 3:   *You can only tell if something is true if you or somebody sees it with their own eyes and ears. That is why there are many people think things are true, like ghosts or witches, that sort of thing. But you might be wrong, so you have to check it first before you say it's true.*

Child 4:   *It's not true because you say it is, but it might be.*

If Howard Gardner (1999) is right that the human mind contains many forms of intelligence, then philosophical intelligence (what he calls 'existential intelligence') may be one of these. All humans have the capacity to ask and respond to existential questioning about ideas and conceptual problems – 'Why?' 'How do you know?' 'What do you mean by...?' These questions lie at the heart of talking for thinking. Such talk involves processing information at the literal level and trying to find deeper meaning at a conceptual level, for example, by asking questions such as 'What is love?', 'What is truth?', 'What is beauty?' But can children engage in this kind of questioning?

What research into P4C has shown is that even young children have the capacity to engage in philosophic questioning, like Tom, age 5, who asked: 'Where does time go when it stops?' Tom may not of course fully understand his question, but he is full of curiosity and wonder. This capacity to question lies at the heart of intelligent behaviour. But as he gets older it is likely that Tom will ask fewer questions in school. However, the practice of P4C would help to sustain and develop his ability to question and interrogate the world. It has a well-researched pedagogy called 'community of enquiry' and teaching programmes through which the habits of intelligent behaviour can be developed. These habits will help them face the conceptual problems and conflicts that face them in an uncertain world. An eight-year-old expressed the problem we all face: 'The trouble is people are telling you different things, and sometimes your mind tells you to do different things too!'

Gardner (1999) argues that 'students should probe with sufficient depth a manageable set of examples so that they come to see how one thinks and acts in the manner of a scientist, a geometer, an artist, an historian'. In terms of philosophical intelligence, this means showing students what it is like to think and act as a critical speaker, listener and thinker. Michael Ross is a teacher who has used P4C with his primary school classes for many years. He does this, he says:

for the simple reason that philosophy in itself is one of the basic activities of human beings – the questions about life. 'Why are we here?', 'What is it all about?', 'What ought I to do?', etc. may be ignored due to the pressures of everyday life but they are all ultimately addressed by everyone at various periods throughout their lives.

The following are some of the questions raised by a group of Year 3 and 4 children (seven- to nine-year-olds) who had asked if they could discuss God at their next philosophy session in the community of enquiry.[6] The questions reflect the breadth of their vision and imagination:

- Who made God?
- Who is God?
- How was God made? How old is God?
- How did God make the world?
- Why was God made?
- Is God real?
- How did He make us?
- What does Heaven look like?
- Why is God so special?
- Why does God make thunder?
- Why did God make us?
- Why did God make the devil?
- Why does God kill us?
- Why did God make swear words?

The unique value of P4C is that it is the only well-researched thinking approach that focuses specifically on developing questioning, and in particular the kinds of questioning that enable them to think and act with philosophical intelligence.

Collaborating in thoughtful discussion

A community of enquiry seeks to create the optimal conditions for group discussion. One of the prime benefits of this is that it helps children to internalise the ground rules for intelligent discussion. Recent research shows how important this process is in children's thinking. One study describes how teaching the ground rules for effective discussion helped groups to solve non-verbal reasoning test problems. These same children then did statistically better than matching control classes at individual non-verbal reasoning tests.[7] Simply learning how to discuss in reasonable and reflective ways seems to help improve children's reasoning and problem-solving skills.

What is important is to establish the ground rules for such discussion. One teacher did this by listing and discussing with the children all the 'talking' words they could think of, such as 'argument', 'discussion' and 'reason'. The children in groups then discussed and agreed the meaning of each word (with the help of dictionaries and thesauruses). Then they discussed in groups 'the most important rules that people talking in groups should follow' and were asked to come up with no more than six of these. They then discussed as a class the different sets of rules and agreed a final list to display in the classroom, which was:

Our rules for talking and listening

We only talk one at a time.

We all listen to the speaker.

We respect what people say – no 'put downs'.

We try to give reasons for what we say.

We say what we mean.

We can disagree and say 'Why?'

The aims of P4C focus not only on questioning, but on developing discussion and thinking skills. The discussion skills that underlie any learning conversation are also the skills that underpin the National Curriculum in England (DfEE 2000), namely information-processing, enquiry, reasoning, creative thinking and evaluation. P4C provides opportunities for developing all these skills in the following ways.

Information-processing skills: through seeking the meaning of concepts and ideas and using precise language to express what we think. 'Philosophy is good,' as Paul, age 10, said, 'because it helps you understand what you mean.' Information is sought during discussion by use of questions such as: 'What do we know from this?', 'What do we not know?', 'What do we need to know?'

Enquiry skills: through asking relevant questions, posing problems, and engaging in a process of serious and sustained investigation. Enquiry is facilitated during philosophical enquiry by questions such as: 'What do we want to find out?', 'What question(s) do we want to ask?', 'What are the problems?'

Reasoning skills: through reading, discussion and writing to draw inferences and make deductions, give reasons for opinions. As Carl, age 11, said: 'Philosophy helps me to give reasons and explain what I mean.' Reasoning is encouraged by questions such as: 'What can we infer?', 'Are there good reasons for believing it?', 'Can we explain what it means?'

Creative thinking skills: through being playful with ideas, suggesting possible hypotheses, apply imagination to their thinking, and to look for alternative explanations and ideas. As Ravi, age 10, says: 'It can be fun playing with ideas, like thinking impossible things and wondering if they are impossible.' Creativity is encouraged by questions such as: 'Can we build on that idea?', 'Is there another possible viewpoint?', 'How could it be different?'

Evaluation skills: through applying their own judgement to contestable issues, develop criteria for judging the value of ideas, evaluate the ideas and contributions of others, and practise being self-critical and self-correcting. As Paula, age 13, said: 'Philosophy gives you the confidence to speak and think for yourself.' Evaluation can be guided by questions such as: 'What have we learned from this enquiry?', 'How has our thinking changed?', 'What do we still need to think about?'

P4C integrates all these aspects of thinking into one process. Nothing achieves these ends more effectively than open-ended group discussions of ideas and questions in which young people are interested, assisted by a philosophically aware teacher.

Being critical and creative

What philosophical enquiry offers is a tried and tested strategy for helping children apply critical and creative reasoning to stories and other texts. The teaching strategy, which is based on whole-class discussion, is called 'community of enquiry'. It is not a new strategy, but one that is gaining popularity, because it works in making children more reflective and critical readers. Teachers in more than 30 countries find that philosophy is adding value to the primary curriculum by providing a 'Fourth R' – Reasoning – to the basic curriculum. In Brazil alone more than 30,000 children are involved in P4C programmes that are helping to raise standards of literacy.

How does P4C work in the classroom? Ideally, the group sits in a circle or horseshoe, the aim being that everyone can see everyone else. The following are typical stages in a lesson.

A P4C talking to think lesson format[8]

Focusing exercise: sharing the learning objectives, reminding the agreed rules, and using a relaxation exercise or thinking game to ensure alert yet relaxed attention.

Sharing a stimulus: presenting a story, poem, picture or other stimulus for thinking.

Thinking time: children think of what is strange, interesting or unusual about the stimulus and share their thoughts with a partner.

Questioning: children ask their own (or partner's) questions which are written on a board, these are discussed and one is chosen to start the enquiry.

Discussion: children are asked to respond, building on each other's ideas, with the teacher probing for reasons, examples and alternative viewpoints.

Plenary: review the discussion (e.g. using a graphic map), invite last words from children to reflect on the discussion, making links to real situations and possible 'homework'.

Children tend to expect to have their questions unequivocally answered by grown-ups, not discussed by other children. They are often not used to having their attention focused on a particular issue for a length of time, to discuss questions in a systematic and sustained way or to consider things from a variety of viewpoints. But if they have a stimulus (e.g. a story), then even young children can respond to questions in ways that can be called philosophical. This may mean helping them to move from the concrete and literal aspects of the story to the conceptual and the abstract, moving the discussion from *what* happened in the story and *why* to thinking about *what it means.*

Discussion can be moved to philosophical levels through use of Socratic questions (Fisher 2001). Socratic questioning means using a series of questions to progressively engage higher levels of thinking – including literal, analytical and conceptual levels of thinking. The following are examples of questions that engage these three levels of thinking:

1. Literal (or factual) questions ask for information
What is this about?
Can you remember what happened?
What do you have to do?

> **2. Analytic questions call for critical and creative thinking**
> What question(s) do you have?
> What reasons can you give?
> What are the problems/possible solutions here?
>
> **3. Conceptual questions call for abstract thinking**
> What is the key concept (strategy or rule) here and what does it mean?
> What criteria are we using to judge this (or test if it is true)?
> How might we further investigate this concept (strategy or hypothesis)?

This excerpt of discussion of the story 'The Monkey and Her Baby' (Fisher 1999) with six- to seven-year-olds shows the teacher trying to move the children's thinking on through Socratic questioning:

Teacher: *Why did the mother think that her baby was best?*

Child 1: *Because it was beautiful. She thought it was beautiful.*

Child 2: *She thought it was beautiful because she was the mother.*

Teacher: *What does it mean to be beautiful?*

Child 1: *It means someone thinks you are lovely.*

Child 2: *You are perfect…*

Child 1: *Good to look at.*

Teacher: *Can you be beautiful even if no-one thinks you are lovely?*

Child 1: *No. You can't be beautiful if no-one thinks you are beautiful.*

Child 2: *You can be beautiful inside, you can feel beautiful…*

Paul, a reluctant reader, age 8, suddenly sees the point of it all during a philosophical discussion of a story: 'Oh, I get it! We're not supposed to just read the story. We're supposed to think about it.' For him, it is a revelation. Although still struggling with the mechanics of reading, he finds he is able to make a personal response, to question, to discuss inferences and meanings using challenging texts during the shared reading session. For John, age 10, philosophy not only gives him time to think in a serious, structured and sustained way, but also: 'It helps you ask questions. It shows you there can be many answers to one question [and] it makes you think that everything must have a reason.' For Michelle, age 10, the community of enquiry gives you a chance to self-correct your thinking. She says: 'In philosophy lessons you can say what you really think and sometimes you change your mind.'

It is not only children who find 'the philosophy effect' stimulating and challenging. An increasing number of teachers build regular philosophy sessions into their literacy work, and report encouraging results. The national organisation for the use of philosophy with children (SAPERE) report evidence from Ofsted inspections that have praised the role of philosophical discussion in raising standards of literacy in infant and junior classes (www.sapere.net).

One teacher reports that philosophical discussion has added 'another dimension' to her teaching, one that will provide 'added value' to her Literacy Hour. 'The results for me were truly inspirational,' says Morag Macinnes, 'and show that the approach is suitable for all children ... and shows also that stories and collaborative discussion develop thinking skills.' So what skills are being developed?

The National Literacy Strategy describes shared reading as the class reading together, 'discussing ideas and textual features, engaging in a high level of interaction'. There is no higher level of interaction with children than a philosophical discussion in a community of enquiry. The skills identified in the Literacy Strategy are those routinely developed in a philosophy for children session, including:

- linking the story to personal experience;
- interrogating and evaluating the story;
- identifying themes and ideas;
- distinguishing between opinion and evidence in the text;
- identifying implicit meanings;
- developing a critical reading stance.

Philosophy for children fulfils the criteria for high level discussion of texts, but it offers more. It is about training children not only to answer, but also to ask questions, to interrogate texts, so that they learn how to be not only active, critical readers, but also critical and reasonable thinkers. Research shows that the practice of P4C enables children to obtain higher achievement scores in tests of verbal reasoning. But skills alone are not enough; what must be added to these to make them effective is the awareness of when and how we may use these skills to make a difference. Being reasonable means being more than rational. To be reasonable we need to be mindful of self and others.

Caring – being mindful of self and others

P4C does not overlook the emotional aspects of living and learning together. The community of enquiry creates the conditions that foster emotional engagement and self-expression. It creates conditions that engender awareness of others and new feelings towards them. The child will better understand, refine and control their feelings if he or she can reason, explain and discuss in an optimal way. Discussion in a community of enquiry requires the group to develop trust and the ability to co-operate, and to respect the views of others. They develop insight into the problematical nature of knowledge, and the need to subject what they read, see and hear to critical enquiry. Through this process they develop self-esteem as thinkers and learners.

There are two sets of dispositions or attitudes that philosophy for children aims to foster – being mindful of oneself and of others. Both derive from the dialogical nature of the process, developing individual skills through co-operative activity. P4C pioneer Matthew Lipman calls these aspects 'caring' thinking (Lipman 2003). Caring thinking involves learning to collaborate with others in a community of enquiry, developing empathy and respect for others. It means being guided by questions such as:

- What do others think?
- Can I understand what they think?
- Can I learn from what they think?

By taking part in a community of enquiry, children develop personal qualities such as the need to listen to and respect others, and the self-confidence to speak their mind, challenge others and change their views.

P4C develops and strengthens what Goleman calls 'emotional intelligence'. Studies show that a youngster's life chances are at least as much affected by emotional intelligence, as they are by other aspects of intelligence (Goleman 1997). Emotional intelligence includes:

- *self-awareness* knowing how/what you are feeling and how it impinges on your work, having a realistic awareness of one's abilities;
- *self-regulation* handling emotions so they facilitate the task in hand, being conscientious;
- *resilience* sustaining motivation, persevering in the face of setbacks, striving to improve;
- *empathy* sensing what other people are feeling, and using that information in our dealings with them, being able to have a rapport with a wide range of people;

- *social skills* reading social situations, using skills to persuade, lead and negotiate.

Philosophical discussion can develop all these personal qualities. It does so by making thinking relevant to children's personal needs and quest for answers. It is less a curriculum and more a way of life. It has more to do with what the Greeks called *phronesis* (practical wisdom) than it has to do with *tekne* (skills), more to do with the intellectual behaviour than competence. It is to do with the dispositions to behave intelligently when confronted with problems, uncertainties and puzzling questions. It is about persisting in a task, sustaining the enquiry, pursuing the question. It is about encouraging mindfulness and resisting impulsivity, thinking before acting, allowing others their say. It is about listening with understanding and empathy, devoting mental energy to attending to what others say, perceiving other points of view and sensing their emotions. It is about the metacognitive capacity to know oneself, to be aware of one's own thoughts and feelings and their effects on others.

John Stuart Mill argued we do not learn to read and write, to ride or swim merely by being told how to do it; we learn by doing it – similarly, only by involving children in democratic processes of discussion and decision-making will they ever learn how to practise it (Fisher 2003). In a democratic society, beliefs must be self-accepted rather than uncritically imbibed, freely chosen rather than externally imposed. The nurturing of the 'reasonable person' lies at the heart of education in citizenship.

The exercise of philosophical enquiry is, like any educative practice, most effective when it is participatory, proactive, communal, collaborative and given over to constructing meanings rather than receiving them. P4C, with its emphasis on inclusive, democratic practice, provides a powerful means for children to share experience and explore meaning. They can learn to express their views with confidence, to raise doubts and questions, and to challenge the thinking of others. Through engaging in a community of enquiry children learn how to do the following:

- ask their own questions and raise issues for discussion;
- explore and develop their own ideas, views and theories;
- give reasons for what they think and believe;
- explain and argue their point of view with others;
- listen to and consider the views and ideas of others;
- change their ideas in the light of good reasons and evidence.

The oral nature of P4C is crucial to its radical democratic role. Children are swamped by written and visual information. They need to be given a voice, a voice to question, to challenge, to construct and deconstruct the meanings around them. As Jason, age 10, says, 'Everyone is telling you things and not getting you to think things through.' P4C is a way to engage critically with their given world, and to find a space to think things through. Like other groups in society, such as women, ethnic minorities and the poor, children's views have been marginalised and their claims to knowledge and to reason have been devalued. P4C opens up a space for thinking, for sharing beliefs and for creating knowledge, as in the following excerpt from a discussion by a group of nine-year-olds on whether it is right for parents to smack their children:

Child: *I think Sophie's was a good idea why smacking children is wrong.*

Teacher: *What was the idea?*

Child: *Well, she said it was wrong because smacking you doesn't tell you why it was wrong, it just tells you that if you do it, you will get smacked. That means you'll do it again if you can get away with it and not be smacked. But if you are told why it is wrong ... whatever it is ... then you are less likely to do it again. Because you know why it is wrong. If you understand the reason ...*

P4C has been shown to be an effective approach in teaching democratic community values (Fisher 2003). It gives children a voice and a vote in deciding the focus and the course of the enquiry. P4C offers an arena for the free flow of their views, a space for creativity and dialogue.

Some final thoughts

P4C does not just provide a 'talking shop', or an exercise in free-flowing discussion. Research suggests that programmes that promote thinking skills have positive effects on academic achievement.[9] The research evidence from a wide range of small-scale studies across the world indicates that the philosophy for children's programmes can make a difference to various aspects of a child's academic performance. Findings from my Philosophy in Primary Schools research project echo worldwide research into P4C programmes and show positive effects on the following:

- pupils' achievements in academic tests;
- children's self-esteem and self-concept as thinkers and learners;
- the fluency and quality of children's questioning;
- the quality of their creative thinking and verbal reasoning;
- their ability to listen to others and engage effectively in class discussion.

Research shows the positive effects of philosophical discussion extend across the curriculum.[10] As Jemma, age 10, said: 'Philosophy can help in all your lessons, no matter what you're learning.'

Teachers generally feel that philosophical discussion adds a new dimension to their teaching and the way their pupils think. Children become more ready to ask questions, to challenge each other and to explain what they mean. As Kim, age 9, put it: 'The important thing is not to agree or disagree but to say why.' Children value what P4C has to offer, not only as a stimulus to learning in the classroom, but also as a life skill. As Camilla, age 10, put it: 'Philosophy helps you make the most of your mind.'

A caveat

It can be challenging when children are encouraged to think for themselves. Uncomfortable consequences can arise from developing philosophical habits in children. This was illustrated for me at the end of a community of enquiry with Year 2 children (six-year-olds). We had been discussing their chosen question after a Story for Thinking lesson when the discussion dried up. I then posed the class a question that I hoped might further stimulate their philosophical thinking. 'How do you know I am Mr Fisher?' I asked. There was silence. This is good, I thought, for they are really thinking this through. The silence dragged on and I began to wonder whether any of the class would respond. Suddenly a child's hand went up. 'How do you know *you're* Mr Fisher?' he asked.

When children develop the habits of intelligent behaviour, the results can be unpredictable. When they learn how to interrogate ideas within texts and in the world, they will also learn to interrogate you and what you say. Talking for thinking with children is an intellectual adventure that may be full of unexpected challenges.

Notes

1. Philosophy for Children is a programme for teaching thinking developed by Matthew Lipman (Lipman 1981). It has since been adapted and developed for use in many countries (Fisher 2003).
2. For a recent survey of research, see Trickey and Topping (2004).
3. For a useful summary of classroom research, see Alexander (2004).
4. A trend noted in Dillon (1988).
5. For the story 'Mercury and the Axe', and further questions and suggestions on ways of using the story to create a community of enquiry, see Fisher (1999: 45) and other books in the *Stories for Thinking* series.
6. I am indebted to Julie Winyard for this example. See also Winyard (2005), which has further examples of P4C dialogue with her class of Y3 and Y4 pupils.

7. See Wegerif (2002). For more on his 'Thinking Together' approach, see www.thinkingtogether.org.uk
8. For other descriptions of the stages of a P4C lesson, see Cleghorn (2002), Haynes (2002) and Robert Fisher's *Stories for Thinking* series.
9. For reviews of research, see McGuiness (1999), and Fisher (2005a, 2005b).
10. In a recent study a three-year thinking programme, including a P4C, resulted in a school getting its best ever English test results (Fisher 2005a). See also Dyfed (1994).

References and further reading

Alexander, R. (2004) *Towards Dialogic Teaching*. Cambridge: Dialogos.

Cleghorn, P. (2002) *Thinking through Philosophy*. Blackburn: Education Printing Services.

DfEE (2000) *The National Curriculum: Handbook for Primary Teachers in England*. London: DfEE.

Dillon, J.T. (1988) *Questioning and Teaching*. London: Routledge.

Dyfed Local Education Authority (1994) *The Improving Reading Standards in Primary Schools Project Report*. Camarthen: Dyfed LEA.

Fisher, R. (1996) *Stories for Thinking*. Oxford: Nash Pollock.

Fisher, R. (1997a) *Games for Thinking*. Oxford: Nash Pollock.

Fisher, R. (1997b) *Poems for Thinking*. Oxford: Nash Pollock.

Fisher, R. (1999) *First Stories for Thinking*. Oxford: Nash Pollock.

Fisher, R. (2000) *First Poems for Thinking*. Oxford: Nash Pollock.

Fisher, R. (2001) *Values for Thinking*. Oxford: Nash Pollock.

Fisher, R. (2003) *Teaching Thinking: Philosophical Enquiry in the Classroom* (2nd edn). London: Continuum.

Fisher, R. (2005a) *Teaching Children to Learn* (2nd edn). Cheltenham: Nelson Thornes.

Fisher, R. (2005b) *Teaching Children to Think* (2nd edn). Cheltenham: Nelson Thornes.

Fisher, R. and Williams, M. (eds) (2004) *Unlocking Creativity: Teaching Across the Curriculum*. London: David Fulton Publishers.

Fisher, R. and Williams, M. (eds) (2005) *Unlocking Literacy* (2nd edn). London: David Fulton Publishers.

Gardner, H. (1999) *Intelligence Reframed*. New York: Basic Books.

Goleman, D. (1997) *Emotional Intelligence: Why It Can Matter More than IQ*. New York: Bantam Books.

Haynes, J. (2002) *Children as Philosophers*. London: RoutledgeFalmer.

Lipman, M. (1981) 'Philosophy for children', in A.L. Costa (ed.) *Developing Minds: Programs for Teaching Thinking*. Alexandria, VA: Association for Supervision and Curriculum Development.

Lipman, M. (2003) *Thinking in Education*. Cambridge: Cambridge University Press.

McGuiness, C. (1999) *From Thinking Skills to Thinking Classrooms: A Review and Evaluation of Approaches for Developing Pupils' Thinking*. Research Report No. 115. London: DfES.

Nietzsche, F. (1888) *The Will to Power*.

Trickey, S. and Topping, K.J. (2004) 'Philosophy for children: a systematic review', *Research Papers in Education*, 19(3): 365–80.

Wegerif, R. (2002) 'The importance of intelligent conversations', *Teaching Thinking*, 9: 46–9.

Winyard, J. (2005) 'Cunning little vixens', *Teaching Thinking and Creativity*, Spring 2005: 30–6.

CHAPTER 4

Inclusive approaches to communication with children with special educational needs

Nicola Grove

The focus of this chapter is the use of strategies to promote effective communication for children who have special educational needs (SEN). Children with special educational needs have always been educated in mainstream classrooms, whether or not they were labelled as such, and for many years teachers have differentiated their approaches to suit children with different aptitudes, interests and needs. So teaching for inclusion is nothing new – it's always been there. However, it is true to say that in the twenty-first century our understanding of differing needs is structured in a particular way that makes specific demands on teaching staff, and that there are challenges and possibilities inherent in the current system for children who learn and interact with others in unorthodox ways. We know that school staff are positive and committed to the principle of inclusion, but that many feel that they lack a basic understanding of language and communication, and also the specialist knowledge needed to make inclusion work.[1]

Traditionally, special needs were defined in medical terms, which needed remediation on an individual basis. As a reaction, some radical approaches to inclusion disregard the contribution of impairments and developmental processes within the child, and view special needs as purely socially constructed.[2] More recently there has been a recognition that we need to take account of three principal dimensions of inclusion: (1) what the child brings; (2) the skills and attitudes of those who interact with the child; and (3) the context within which the child functions.[3]

Who are children with special educational needs?

Current estimates (DfES 2005) suggest that, overall, 15 per cent of the pupil population are likely to have SEN, although only 3 per cent will have statements.

In the primary sector, the figure is higher (16.5 per cent) than in the secondary sector (14.3 per cent). This means that in an average class of 30 children, we might expect there to be around 5 with special needs. Of course, not all of these needs are necessarily long term. The needs are defined as those which affect a child's ability to learn and function well in the school community: cognitive and learning needs; language and communication needs; social emotional needs; sensory needs; and physical needs.

The underlying causes of SEN may include such examples as an extreme emotional response to a life event, or a physical condition resulting from a temporary but debilitating illness as well as permanent conditions such as deafness, autistic spectrum disorder or Down syndrome. These categories are identified through the annual schools census of pupil levels, and are the officially recognised descriptors of conditions.

The needs of some children will be relatively clear-cut, but many children may have more than one underlying impairment or disability. Some may have several educational needs arising from the primary condition which will affect their education in complex ways. For example, children with Down syndrome and learning difficulties are almost certain to have some degree of hearing impairment; children with cerebral palsy (a physical condition) are likely to have complex visual problems which will affect their ability to handle visual tasks, say, in mathematics and geography.[4] However, research and practice over the past ten years or so provide strong evidence that teachers and classroom staff should not feel overwhelmed by the diversity and complexity of conditions that affect children in their care. When categories of educational need are linked to the categories of descriptors from the Pupils' Level Annual School Census (PLASC),[5] there is a great deal of overlap. We know that adopting some general principles and strategies seem to work well for all pupils – and not just those with special educational needs.

Communication and SEN

It is evident that communication difficulties are among the most common educational needs arising from a range of different conditions. This is because communication and language themselves involve many different and complex processes. Any act of communication involves every aspect of our bodies. We use our faces, eyes, hands, whole bodies as well as our speech organs to express ourselves, and even small anomalies in any one of these behaviours can have quite profound effects. If you look someone too long in the eye, or don't look at them at all; if you stand too close or too far away; if you speak too slowly or too fast; if you persistently misread emotional signals – you are likely to disrupt an exchange just as much as if you fail to hear what is said, or cannot find the right words to express yourself. The upside is that there are many ways in which you

Table 4.1 Categories of special educational need

Specific learning difficulties (SPLD)	Particular difficulties with reading, writing, spelling or number. May also have problems with memory, organisation and co-ordination; includes children with dyslexia, dyscalculia and dyspraxia (developmental co-ordination difficulties).
Moderate learning difficulties (MLD)	Pupils who achieve significantly below expected levels of the curriculum, whose needs cannot be met through normal differentiation and flexibility in teaching.
Severe learning difficulties (SLD)	Pupils with significant cognitive impairments which affect their access to the curriculum. They are likely to have additional problems in communication, self-help, motor skills and perception.
Profound and multiple learning difficulties (PMLD)	Pupils with severe, multiple and complex learning needs, often combined with sensory or motor impairments and health conditions. Pupils are dependent on others for learning and personal care.
Behavioural, emotional and social difficulties (BESD)	Pupils who have difficulties with social interaction. They may have poor concentration, find it hard to inhibit responses and have low self-esteem. They may show challenging behaviour, or may be withdrawn and passive, or may show overactive and impulsive behaviours.
Speech, language and communication needs (SLCN)	Pupils with specific difficulties in the development and use of speech, communication and language.
Autistic spectrum disorder (ASD)	Pupils with specific difficulties in understanding and using verbal and non-verbal communication, social behaviour and flexible thinking and behaviour.
Visual impairment (VI)	Pupils with visual difficulties or blindness which requires adaptations to the environment and curriculum
Hearing impairment (HI)	Pupils who have hearing losses, ranging from mild to severe to profound
Multisensory impairment (MSI)	Pupils who have a significant combination of hearing and visual impairments, including deafblindness.
Physical disabilities (PD)	Pupils with physical impairments which impact on their access to education – may include mobility issues or the use of communication aids.

can compensate for a difficulty in one particular area, provided that the people you interact with are sensitive and responsive and the environment in which you are communicating is facilitative. Both speaking and listening are processes that are highly vulnerable to disruption – because auditory signals are fast, transitory and decay quickly (therefore hard to remember and store, even if you have very good hearing) – and production of intelligible speech requires very fine co-ordination of breath, lips, tongue and palate.

Total communication

One of the first things we have to do when considering how to unlock speaking and listening for an inclusive school is to redefine the terms. The trouble with 'speaking and listening', as a label for direct face-to-face communication, is that for children who cannot speak orally, or listen aurally, it does not seem relevant. It also, rather unhelpfully, emphasises the end points in an act of communication, rather than the central processes whereby messages are understood and generated. For children with special needs, it may be more helpful to use two more general terms: expression and comprehension, and to think of 'total communication' – that is, the use of all relevant channels of expression and understanding information that are at the child's disposal.

The process of communication

It is useful to consider what actually goes on when people communicate with each other, in order to understand where things can go awry for a child with special needs, and how to help them compensate for their difficulties. A distinction is usually made between two levels of processing information: the first level involving input and output: the senses (hearing, vision, touch, smell, taste) and the motor system (organs of articulation, hands, facial expressions and eye movements, body movements) and the second involving so-called central processes where the brain decodes and encodes meaning, retrieving information from memory and storing new information.

Input processes: perceiving and attending

We first have to actually notice that something is being communicated. This means that the signal has got to be sufficiently prominent, which is arguably the responsibility of the sender rather than the receiver of the message. It may seem obvious, but recent developments in the design of classrooms have emphasised how very maladapted many buildings are for teaching and learning.[6] Many teachers, too, can be helped by learning basic techniques of voice projection and management, since even mild voice problems seem to affect children's ability to process information.[7]

Understanding requires us to pay attention to what is being communicated. Attention involves focusing, sustaining concentration, executing an action, and shifting between different tasks.[8] This usually involves listening – but for a deaf child it would require watching and for a blind and deaf child, attending to a tactile signal. The point about attention is that it involves very active selection of a stimulus. We now know that the brain has an incredible capacity to screen out information that is irrelevant or uninteresting, so that even in noisy surroundings we can hear the words 'I love you' or 'Would you like another drink?' Selective attention is something that develops with age, and which may have to be specifically taught to children with SEN – it does not come automatically. Of course, lack of attention may be the result of boredom, or insubordination, or laziness but it is just as likely to result from a primary difficulty in screening out distractions or in understanding what is being said, or perhaps from hunger, tiredness or emotional or physical discomfort. Children who look away while being spoken to, may be neither insubordinate nor bored, but trying to process what is being said.[9]

CASE STUDY: THINK AGAIN ABOUT INATTENTION

Jamie, age 9, was always the first to put his hand up, talked loudly over other children and could rarely remember what had been said to him. Through discussion with his class teacher, Jamie identified that one of the main difficulties he had in class was with listening. We went through possible causes with him, and Jamie indicated that the problem was not boredom or lack of wanting to listen, but that he often could not hear what was said. A hearing test was arranged and Jamie was found to have an undiagnosed loss which meant he could not hear speech at a conversational level if there was ambient noise.

Even if children are attending fully, they may have difficulties in understanding because of problems with their receptive language system, or comprehension. This brings us to consideration of central processes.

Central processes: the language system

Generally, we make a distinction between *language* and *communication*, with communication being the broader process whereby people exchange both verbal and non-verbal messages, whereas language denotes the aspects of that message which are formally codified in a symbolic system. A distinction is also made between *language* and *speech* – with speech being only one of the ways in which language is realised. We now know, for example, that sign languages – which do not involve the vocal channel – share all the characteristics of spoken language systems, namely a grammar, a vocabulary and socially codified rules for their expression, or pragmatics. These aspects of the language system are sometimes referred to as Form, Content and Use or pragmatics:

- *Form*: languages are made up of patterns of elements – sounds in speech – which come together to make words and sentences and paragraphs. So the formal aspect of language covers both the structure of sounds (*phonology*), words (their *morphology*) and sentences (*syntax*). A child who has difficulties with the formal aspects of language may have difficulty perceiving certain sounds, may leave out word endings, simplify long words, or find it hard to understand and/or produce complex sentences.

- *Content* is the term used to denote vocabulary and meanings, the semantics of the language. This covers the kind of words that we use – whether abstract (*glory, failure*) or concrete (*chair, cat*); the classes of words we use (nouns, adjectives, adverbs, verbs, etc.); and the way that words and meanings relate to each other (*king, prince, kingdom, govern, ruler; pen, pencil, rubber, draw, ruler*). Children who have difficulties with these aspects of language may find it difficult to learn new words, and may have limited vocabularies. They may not be able to recall the right word quickly and use lots of 'filler' words such as *um, er*, or hesitations or long-winded non-specific 'circumlocutions'. In addition, they may over-use general terms such as 'that', 'thing', 'got', 'do' and may find it hard to acquire abstract language.

- *Use* or *pragmatics* refers to the social use of both the content and the form of language. It covers the ways in which communication functions to perform certain social acts (such as *promising, insulting, begging, arguing, loving*) and the cultural conventions which dictate which forms and which meanings will be used in a particular social context – for example, the difference between greeting a close teenage friend and a Member of Parliament. Use of language also involves non-verbal aspects such as intonation, prosody and body language. Pragmatics is critically important in informing our understanding of children who have difficulty with the social aspects of language. This may be due to several factors, e.g.: lack of experience of certain conventions and contexts; emotional issues; the fact that they cannot hear or see properly; or difficulties in working out what other people are feeling and thinking.

These children may appear rude, shy or passive; may give too much or too little information; may fail to understand or use non-literal meanings or seem very pedantic in their choice of words. Non-verbal aspects may be affected, so that their speech sounds wooden or mechanical. In some cases, they may stand too close or too far away when they talk to another person.

Form, content and use are all involved in both comprehension (receptive language) and expression (expressive language). The relationship between comprehension and expression varies in children with SEN. In normal development, comprehension is in advance of expression, so that we generally assume that children can understand more than they say. In some children they will be about equal, and in others, comprehension may actually be lower than expected from the way they talk. An illustration of this is provided in the following case study.

CASE STUDY: COMPREHENSION AND EXPRESSION IN CHILDREN WITH SEN

Susie is 5 years old and has cerebral palsy. She has no intelligible speech and uses a communication board with pictures and words which she points to; she also uses a lot of gesture and facial expression to get her message across. Her understanding is actually at a 6 year level – i.e. in advance not only of expression, but also of her chronological age. People who do not know Susie assume that she has only limited understanding, and tend to talk to her as though she were much younger. This annoys her a lot!

Michael is 7 years old and has hydrocephalus and spina bifida. He talks all the time, using full sentences. People therefore think that he understands complex sentences. However, if you listen carefully to Michael talking, he is using a lot of 'learned phrases' – like 'I was only thinking the other day', 'the point is…' 'we had a great time, didn't we?' In fact, his understanding of language is at about the average of a four-and-a-half-year-old child. In conversation or instruction he needs short sentences, and a lot of time to process information. However, in drama and in literature, he will enjoy listening to and using rich language with lots of rhythm and intonation.

Central processes: memory

Both short-term (working) memory and long-term (storage) memory are involved in processing language. Working memory has been defined as 'the mental workplace in which information can be temporarily stored and manipulated during complex everyday activities'.[10] The system involves an executive element which retrieves items from long-term memory and manages the task of sorting all the information which is arriving simultaneously; a system which holds in place the incoming sounds of speech so that they can be processed, and an element that does the same for visuo-spatial information. Long-term memory stores meanings and the way these are represented (whether in words, gestures or facial movements) and this system interacts with and is updated through working memory. There is considerable evidence that working memory and difficulties with auditory processing of information underlie many of the language difficulties, in both vocabulary and grammar, that children demonstrate in the classroom. These include: the ability to follow, understand and produce grammatical structures (Bishop 1997), the ability to acquire new words (Baddeley *et al.* 1998), the ability to discriminate between similar sounding words, and the ability to recall information presented through the auditory channel (Gathercole and Pickering 2001)

Output processes

Once we have understood an incoming message, we may (or may not!) construct a reply. In order to do this, a meaning and intention are generated centrally, and the appropriate words and sentence forms are assigned. We then have to actually articulate the message – through speech, gestures, face and body. In asking a question, for example, we not only formulate the sentence; we have to use a particular intonation, and may adjust our body language accordingly. Some children with special needs could have primary difficulties at the level of motor output which means that their speech is unclear. Many children take some time to develop the complex sound systems of the language (typically, the earliest sounds to be produced are ones like *m, b, w, l*, whereas sounds which require more complex co-ordination come later: *th, r, s*). Children with underlying physical co-ordination problems may continue to have difficulties producing sounds; single words and short phrases may be clear but sentences are not. Other children may show problems in producing clear hand gestures or the use of facial muscles – typically children with some form of cerebral palsy or severe dyspraxia (sometimes called developmental motor difficulties).

Communication and other skills

It is now well recognised that a firm foundation in communication is needed for children to achieve their potential in both social and academic aspects of their education. Children with an inadequate grasp of vocabulary will be hampered as they face increasingly complex and abstract concepts in different subjects[11] and children with poor language skills will find it difficult to master literacy.[12] Most importantly, without effective communication, it is difficult to make friends, collaborate and learn from others, or to gain a sense of oneself as a valued member of a social group.

Difficulties and skills in communication for children with SEN

Although there is no one-to-one correspondence between an identified condition or disability and single communication problems, there are nevertheless some communication difficulties that are consistently associated with some conditions. It is critical to remember that we are talking about predictions, not certainties, and that children have an extraordinary capacity to surprise.

CASE STUDY: WATCH YOUR PRECONCEPTIONS! THE CASE OF JOHNNY

I met Johnny at a storytelling festival where I was on the bookstall. Aged about 9 or 10, he had Down syndrome and was there with his mum and brother. He was looking intently through the books and tapes. I asked him if he was enjoying the festival and he said yes he was. I asked which stories he had enjoyed most, but he misunderstood and thought I was asking about his usual favourites. Children with Down syndrome have auditory processing difficulties and comprehension problems so you might expect him to like picture stories suitable for younger children. His best stories though were the Iliad and the Odyssey as told for adults by Hugh Lupton, a well-known oral storyteller. He listened to the tapes over and over again and could recite them by heart.

Children with autistic spectrum disorders

Autistic spectrum disorders (ASD) tend to be associated with fundamental difficulties in communication, in understanding other people's emotions, and social conventions. Their thinking tends to lack flexibility and 'central coherence' – that is, the ability to see things as a whole and to disengage from specifics. In addition, they are inclined to show rigid preferences for routines and familiar structures and to find change and transition difficult. Children with ASD may have moderate or severe learning difficulties, but around one-third have an IQ within the normal range for their ages. Use of language and social understanding are particular problems for children with ASD. Children can be helped by clear expectations, visual cues as to what will happen, structure and routine and explicit information about what they should do and why things are happening.[13] Traditionally, it was thought that children with ASD would not be able to play symbolically or participate in imaginative activities, but the ground-breaking work of Sherratt and Peter,[14] among others, has shown that this is not actually the case.

Speech and Language Impairments (SLI)

These are generally classified into three groups by Broomfield and Dodd:[16]

1 *Receptive group*: children with problems understanding language – nearly always associated with some expressive difficulties as well.

> **CASE STUDY: DRAMA AND PLAY WITH AUTISTIC CHILDREN**
>
> Jem tended to poke other children and behave unpredictably; he had several mannerisms such as flapping and stamping. He was mainly interested in mechanical objects, especially washing machines. He showed some limited symbolic understanding, e.g. pushing a box along the table and saying 'brrm'. His teacher used a highly structured drama approach to develop his ability to take part with other children in role play – by putting him in charge of a 'machine' (cardboard box) and getting him to ask them for items of clothing to sort and put in the machine on 'washing day'. This led to increased social play for Jem, who began to be included in more classroom activities where he could ask for and give objects.[15]

2 *Expressive group*: children whose main difficulties are in expressing themselves. Understanding is in advance of, or equal to, expression.

3 *Speech impairment group*: difficulties in articulating words and sentences.

In Broomfield and Dodd's study, there was a great deal of overlap in the problems experienced by these children. In the receptive group, virtually all had problems with expressive language structure (grammar) and with the development of vocabulary (two-thirds had difficulties with speech production as well). In the expressive group, over half also had problems with articulating speech sounds.

For the purposes of diagnosis and statementing, children will only be considered to have SLI if they are deemed to have problems in these areas which *cannot* be attributed to other causes such as learning difficulties, sensory difficulties, emotional or environmental deprivation. Nevertheless, there are many children with other sets of problems who may actually also have specific speech and language difficulties. For example, it is now recognised that children with Down syndrome (hence with a primary categorisation of learning difficulty) share many characteristics with children who have SLI.[17]

Deafness and hearing impairment

Children with hearing impairments are a very heterogeneous group, with somewhat different needs, depending on their levels of hearing and the kind of language input they have received early in their lives. Around half of deaf pupils have a moderate or mild loss; half have a severe or profound loss. The ability to hear speech is, however, not predictable from the level of hearing loss alone – much depends on other factors such as environmental noise, familiarity with the incoming information, motivation and health. About one-third of these children have additional SEN. Acceptance of sign language has revolutionised our understanding of the needs of deaf children. Deaf children who are exposed to

CASE STUDY: SPEAKING, LISTENING AND VOCABULARY

Najma and Darren are eight years old and have particular difficulties with vocabulary. They are struggling with some of the concepts they meet in maths tasks, clearly not understanding them or using them. The learning support assistant and speech and language therapist work with them over time. They use a structured approach which is designed to build up the associations and meanings they can generate when they hear terms like *addition, horizontal, amount, equals, between, decrease*. They construct word banks of the new terms, by working through the sound of the word, what rhymes with it, how many meanings there are. Games are played in which words are repeated several times in different contexts. The children are also helped to take control of the process by thinking each time about how to learn and remember new words. The class teacher uses some of these techniques when she introduces new words to the class, and has posters up on the wall with bubbles to show all the meanings of each term, made by the children themselves. Najma and Darren successfully learn and use the target words as a result of this teaching.[18]

fluent sign language from birth seem to develop completely age-appropriate language skills – i.e. the grammar and the semantic system of sign, which is very different from English. Acquisition of sign language is not only a linguistic process, it is a cultural inheritance, involving a shared history and norms of social interaction (Woll and Kyle, in press). On the other hand, children who have not received fluent language models in a form that they can perceive and understand from birth are likely to have severe delays in all aspects of language (whether signed or spoken).

'Deafinitions'

1. Mild deafness
People with mild deafness have some difficulty following speech, mainly in noisy situations. The quietest sounds they can hear in their better ear average between 25 and 39 decibels. A quiet conversation usually averages about 30 decibels.

2. Moderate deafness
People with moderate deafness have difficulty in following speech without a hearing aid. The quietest sounds they can hear in their better ear average between 40 and 69 decibels. A busy shop usually averages about 60 decibels.

3. Severe deafness

People with severe deafness rely a lot on lipreading, even when they have a hearing aid. British Sign Language (BSL) may be their first or preferred language. The quietest sounds they can hear in their better ear average between 70 and 94 decibels. A city street usually averages about 70 decibels.

4. Profound deafness

People who are profoundly deaf communicate by lipreading. BSL may be their first or preferred language. The quietest sounds they can hear in their better ear average 95 decibels or more. An underground railway usually averages about 90 decibels, while a pneumatic drill generally averages about 100 decibels.

Source: http://www.rnid.org.uk/mediacentre/

The communication needs of the deaf or hearing impaired child are profoundly affected by the educational approach which is adopted in their school. Gregory (2005)[19] describes the continuum of approaches, from the purely aural-oral which emphasises the use of residual hearing to master speech and English as the primary language, to sign bilingual approaches, where deaf children are taught together in sign and learn English as a second language. In the middle are hybrid approaches, where, for example, deaf children are taught alongside hearing children using the services of a sign interpreter, or where teachers use English but accompany it with some signing. This latter approach has been found to be highly ineffective, rather like trying to teach English through using French words with English grammar. The picture for deaf and hearing impaired children is changing very rapidly with the advent of cochlear implantation, a surgical intervention which provides an artificial inner ear. Children with implants, however, do not automatically and immediately process speech as a hearing child would do, and may need sensitive management and teaching to learn to listen effectively.[20]

What works – the inclusive classroom

There is increasing recognition that if we modify the way we teach pupils and adapt the classroom environment in certain fairly simple ways, we can address the learning needs of all pupils. For example, Martin[22] argues that adopting generic strategies to support comprehension and expression is relevant to pupils with SLI. Tallal,[23] reviewing techniques for working with children with SLI, suggests that although they may occasionally need teaching specific skills in isolation, it is absolutely vital that children learn to apply these skills in the

CASE STUDY: HOW TEACHER-TALK HELPS CHILDREN TO SPEAK AND LISTEN

Marla has a severe hearing impairment, though with her aids and lipreading she can pick up speech. Her classroom is adapted with a loop system, and she has classroom support with signing for part of the week. The class teacher and many of the children can use signs. However, her teacher is concerned that Marla takes little part in class talk, and even on a one-to-one basis gives minimal answers. The teacher decides to look at her own style of talking to Marla, and tape records about ten minutes of talk. She notices how many questions she is asking and how often they are 'closed' requiring only yes/no answers; that she is dominating the dialogue, allowing few pauses, and that she often accepts an answer that is not correct from Marla in order to keep the conversation going. She realises that she has a real sense of discomfort during these interactions, trying but not succeeding to put Marla at her ease. So she decides to try a different style: she gives Marla time to think of answers; she starts with open questions (*wh*- type) and occasionally prompts her very naturally by starting a sentence and letting Marla complete it. She also tries to relax and make Marla feel that she is really interested in what she has to say. On listening to the second tape she is surprised by how different Marla seems and how much more she is able to contribute.[21]

classroom if they are to use them effectively – and this means that teachers need to support them appropriately. When writing the guidance to support the use of *Speaking, Listening, Learning* (DfES 2005),[24] we used the expertise of practising teachers and speech and language therapists to put together ideas for adapting and teaching language, and modifying the environment.

The following generic principles, if implemented, will support the development of listening and speaking – comprehension and expression – for all children in your class, including those who have SEN. Here are some simple rules for promoting good communication in the classroom:

- clear simple language, avoid complex sentences and instructions;
- visual clues to the meaning of language and to help with memory – gestures and pictures;
- demonstration and modelling of what you want them to do – don't just tell them;
- opportunities to rehearse and recall instructions – use repetition and be consistent;
- always be ready to respond to children's spontaneous learning and communication, build what they give you into your teaching;

- explanation and enrichment of vocabulary and concepts; plan beforehand what vocabulary is needed and how you will teach it;

- a clear structure and predictable ritual to lessons, with different aspects labelled in ways children can understand, e.g. sign/picture for whole-group work; discussion, reading, work on your own, work with a partner;

- acceptance of all appropriate forms of communication;

- alternating tasks which demand attention and listening with physical activity and discussion; emotional support from staff and peers;

- quiet, well-organised environments which are adapted to their physical and learning needs: furniture which is comfortable and the right height;

- availability of drinking water, access to nutritious snacks during the day.

The strategies outlined in this chapter are fundamental to the success of an inclusive policy that seeks to respect the rights of children to be educated in an appropriate neighbourhood school with their local friends, and to take advantage of a broad and rich curriculum. If we can be confident in a pedagogy which supports all learners and recognises the interaction between context, communication and the learner, it will be easier to identify the children who need extra provision to meet their distinct personal needs.

Acknowledgements

I would like to thank the team who put together the SEN materials for speaking, listening and learning: Nick Peacey, Maggie Johnson, Ann Miles, Janeta Guarneri, Jan Pennington, Wendy Rinaldi, Melanie Peter, Claire Topping, Julie Dockrell and Ann Middleton. The ideas in this chapter are largely based on the information and experience they generously provided.

Notes

1. See Sadler (2005).
2. See Oliver (1990); Barton (2003).
3. See Lewis and Norwich (2005).
4. See Stiers *et al.* (2002).
5. More information about PLASC can be found on the website www.teachernet.gov.uk/keywords special educational needs and disabilities.
6. See Shield and Dockrell (2004).
7. See Rogerson and Dodd (2005).
8. See Kelly (2000).
9. See Doherty-Sneddon (2004).
10. See Gathercole and Pickering (2001).
11. See Cummins (1984).
12. Nation and Snowling (2004).

13. See Howlin *et al.* (1998); Gray (2002); Beaney and Kershaw (2003).
14. See Sherratt and Peter (2002).
15. Based on case studies in Sherratt and Peter (2002). The authors show how to develop elaborate social and imaginative drama through careful use of explicit demonstration and a developmentally based approach.
16. See Broomfield and Dodd (2004).
17. Laws and Bishop (2004).
18. Based on Parsons *et al.* (2005). This approach is based on research which suggests that many problems in vocabulary acquisition are to do with limited underlying 'representations' of words in the child's system. By enriching and strengthening the representation of how the word sounds (phonological representations) and the different meanings and associations (semantic representations), learning becomes more secure.
19. Gregory (2005) 'Deafness'.
20. Azar (1998) available at: http://www.apa.org/monitor/apr98/hear.html
21. The teacher had clearly read studies by Wood *et al.* (1986) which demonstrate the difference that adult style of talk had on deaf children's language. These principles seem to hold good for other groups of children with special needs, for example, learning difficulties (Mirenda and Donnellan, 1986) and children with severe cerebral palsy using communication aids and devices (Pennington *et al.* 2004).
22. Martin (2005).
23. Tallal (2000).
24. *Speaking, Listening, Learning: Working with Children Who Have SEN* (DFES 2005). These materials consist of a CD-ROM, including guidance notes, example adaptations of teaching sequences, a video of an example lesson and accompanying posters. They have been developed in light of the increased diversity of needs of children in our classrooms and the emphasis that is rightly placed on the achievement of every individual child. The materials complement *Speaking, Listening, Learning: Working with Children in Key Stages 1 and 2* (DfES0623–2003G) and are intended to support teachers and other staff in developing effective inclusive practice. Reference DfES1187–2005 and DfES1231–2005 to DfES1235–2005. http://www.standards.dfes.gov.uk/primary/publications/inclusion/sll_sen/

References and further reading

Azar, B. (1998) 'Cognitive skills, not just hearing devices, are key to children's ability to hear', *APA Monitor*, 29, 4. Available at: http://www.apa.org/monitor/apr98/hear.html

Baddeley, A.D., Gathercole, S.E. and Papagno, C. (1998) 'The phonological loop as a language learning device', *Psychological Review*, 105: 158–73.

Barton, L. (2003) 'Inclusive Education and Teacher Education', inaugural professorial lecture. London: Institute of Education.

Beaney, J. and Kershaw, P. (2003) *Inclusion in the Primary Classroom: Support Materials for Children with ASD*. London: National Autistic Society.

Bishop, D. (1997) *Uncommon Understanding: Development and Disorders of Language Comprehension in Children*. Hove: Psychology Press.

Broomfield, J. and Dodd, B. (2004) 'Incidence and characteristics of speech language disability', *International Journal of Language and Communication Disorders*, 39: 303–24.

Cummins, J. (1984) *Bilingualism and Special Education: Issues in Assessment and Pedagogy*. Clevedon: Multilingual Matters.

Doherty-Sneddon, G. (2004) 'Don't look now, I'm trying to think: children's eye gaze and cues to comprehension', *The Psychologist*, 17: 82.

Gathercole, S.E. and Pickering, S.J. (2001) 'Working memory deficits in children with special education needs', *British Journal of Special Education*, 28: 89–97.

Gray, C. (2002) *My Social Stories Book*. London: Jessica Kingsley.

Gregory, S. (2005) 'Deafness', in A. Lewis and B. Norwich (eds) *Special Teaching for Special Children: Pedagogies for Inclusion*. Maidenhead: Open University Press.

Howlin, P., Baron-Cohen, S. and Hadwin, J. (1998) *Teaching Children with Autism to Mind-Read: A Practical Guide*. Chichester: Wiley.

Kelly, T.P. (2000) 'The clinical neuropsychology of attention in school-aged children', *Child Neuropsychology*, 6(1): 24–36.

Laws, G. and Bishop, D. (2004) 'Verbal deficits in Down's syndrome and specific language impairment: a comparison', *International Journal of Language and Communication Disorders*, 39: 423–52.

Leonard, L. (1998) *Children with Specific Language Impairment*. Cambridge, MA: MIT Press.

Lewis, A. and Norwich, B. (eds) (2005) *Special Teaching for Special Children: Pedagogies for Inclusion*. Maidenhead: Open University Press.

Martin, D. (2005) 'English as an additional language and children with speech, language and communication needs', in A. Lewis and B. Norwich (eds) *Special Teaching for Special Children: Pedagogies for Inclusion*. Maidenhead: Open University Press.

Mirenda, P.L. and Donnellan, A.M. (1986) 'Effects of adult interaction style in conversational behaviour in students with severe communication problems'. *Language, Speech and Hearing Services in Schools*, 17, 126–41.

Nation, K. and Snowling, M. (2004) 'Beyond phonological skills: broader language skills contibute to the development of reading', *Journal of Research in Reading*, 27(4): 342–56.

Oliver, M. (1990) *The Politics of Disablement*. Basingstoke: Macmillan.

Parsons, S., Law, J. and Gascoigne, M. (2005) 'Teaching receptive vocabulary to children with a speech and language impairment: a curriculum based approach', *Child Language Teaching and Therapy*, 21: 35–59.

Pennington, L., Goldbart, J. and Marshall, J. (2004) 'Interaction training for conversational partners of children with cerebral palsy: a systematic review', *International Journal of Language and Communication Disorders*, 39: 151–70.

Ripley, K., Barrett, J. and Fleming, P. (2001) *Inclusion for Children with Speech and Language Impairment*. London: David Fulton Publishers.

Rogerson, J. and Dodd, B. (2005) 'Is there an effect of dysphonic teachers' voices on children's processing of spoken language?', *Journal of Voice*. 19(1): 47–60.

Sadler, J. (2005) 'Knowledge, attitudes and beliefs of mainstream teachers of children with a preschool diagnosis of SLI', *Child Language Teaching and Therapy*, 21: 147–64.

Sherratt, D. and Peter, M. (2002) *Developing Play and Drama in Children with Autistic Spectrum Disorders*. London: David Fulton Publishers.

Shield, B.M. and Dockrell, J.E. (2004) 'External and internal noise surveys of London primary schools'. *Society and Journal of the Acoustical America*, 115, 730–8.

Stiers, P., Vanderkelen, R., Vanneste, G., Coene, S., De Rammelaere, M. and Vandenbussche, E. (2002) 'Visual-perceptual impairment in a random sample of children with cerebral palsy', *Developmental Medicine and Child Neurology*, 44(6): 370–82.

Tallal, P. (2000) 'Experimental studies of language learning impairments: from research to remediation', in D. Bishop and L. Leonard (eds) *Speech and Language Impairments in Children*. Hove: Psychology Press.

Tallal, P., Bishop, D., Karmiloff-Smith, A. and Karmiloff, K. (2001) *Pathways to Language*. Cambridge, MA: Harvard University Press.

Woll, B. and Kyle, J. (in press) *Sign Language and Deaf Studies*. Cambridge: Cambridge University Press.

Wood, D.J., Wood, H.A., Griffiths, A.J. and Howarth, C.I. (1986) *Teaching and Talking with Deaf Children*. London and New York: Wiley.

Teachers and children: a classroom community of storytellers

Alastair Daniel

Once, when the world was still young...
One day, in a week of two Fridays...
Once, when weeks were as long as months, and years as short as days...
Once upon a time...

There are many ways to begin telling a traditional tale, but the most significant of them all is...by closing the story book. With the current emphasis on developing children's abilities in speaking and listening, this could prove to be a boom time for people, like me, who earn their living by telling stories. However, if storytelling is regarded simply as the preserve of the specialist teller of tales, then I would suggest that those who work in schools will be ignoring one of the most potent tools for classroom teaching.

Although specific references to story and storytelling in the *Speaking, Listening, Learning*[1] objectives are concerned with the child as storyteller, I would maintain that the teacher has an essential role as the principal classroom storyteller. It is my conviction that by experiencing imaginative storytelling, children not only are inspired to become creative and confident in their own tellings, but also experience a sense of engagement that can do nothing but help their development as active and comprehending listeners.

In this chapter, I am, therefore, concerned with developing the teacher's storytelling skills applied not only to the telling of tales, but also across the curriculum. I will outline what I believe are five essential aspects to effective storytelling in the classroom, both in the specific telling of tales and in general teaching. These are:

- the unmediated text – reading or telling?
- narrative storytelling and narrative teaching

- the selection of suitable material
- the adaptation of the story
- the use of 'absence and completion' – engagement and story.

The unmediated text – reading or telling?

Storytelling is a very different thing to *story reading*. With the *Speaking, Listening, Learning* materials there is perhaps an opportunity to justify the listening to and telling of stories as having a value of their own. While it may be excusable that in (what passes for) a literate society, there is a perception that stories are something to be read from a printed or written text, we will happily sit with friends as they regale us with mishaps from their holidays and pay money to listen to the stand-up comedian who creates a whole act from a simple narrative idea (such as buying a pair of shoes). This is storytelling – even though we may not think of it as such – it is the telling of story that is unmediated by a written text and as such it is a fundamental human activity.

I cannot deny the power of reading a book with a group of students, but for many professionals the story book provides a source of protection as much as a source of stories. I cannot imagine that any teacher working in the primary years has not or will not read stories to their class(es), but to put the book down and tell the story is quite another thing: the story told by the storyteller is unmediated – there is no defined text to provide the teller with the words they are going to use. No-one is going to suggest that reading a book with the children is undesirable, let alone wrong, but it is not storytelling and as there is a wealth of material extolling the virtues of using the printed text in the classroom, I will take the opportunity to identify some of the less positive aspects:

- As the reader of a text, you are the voice of the author and not the teller of your own tale. As creative as you may be in your vocal production and use of pace and rhythm, it cannot alter the fact that the printed text is someone else's words.

- The writer of the printed text has aimed their work at a general readership of a particular age (and perhaps even a particular demographic), not your specific pupils. Although words might be changed or phrasing altered, the text leads both reader and hearer down a fixed path that allows little adaptation to the specific group of students.

- The book creates a physical barrier between you and your hearers; even rested across the knees, the paper and cardboard come between teacher and pupils.

- The pictures that form part of most books at this level represent the imaginative response of the illustrator to the narrative, which will not coincide with the response of the children. A picture in effect says: 'We are not talking of your imagined wolf, but the wolf in this picture.'

The *told* story, however, has flexibility and immediacy:

- You can adapt the language to your audience and even incorporate their responses into the story, making the storytelling a unique event for a particular group of pupils and a specific time of telling.
- The absence of a physical object permits freedom of expression for the teller and removes a barrier between you and your hearers.
- It is frequently said 'the best pictures are on radio', and so, as a storyteller, you take your hearers on an imaginary journey that is individual to each one of them as they create characters, settings and encounters in their own heads.

None of the above could possibly justify the exclusion of reading to children, but it does suggest that the story unmediated by a written text also has a place in the classroom.

Narrative storytelling and narrative teaching

One of the defining characteristics of storytelling is the use of narrative and my assertion is that, as storytellers, teachers need to have a grasp of how to construct coherent narratives and exploit their storytelling abilities in giving their teaching a clear narrative form. When I give a lecture on storytelling, I often start with this example: $14 \times 3 = 42$. I ask people to tell me how I solved the problem.

The answer either places me as the subject: 'You took the four and multiplied it by three...'
Or one of the numbers as the subject: 'The three is multiplied by four...'
  But whichever, it includes a character who acts or is acted upon:

>   'First, *you* took the three and multiplied it by four...'
>   'First, *the three* is multiplied by four...'

...a quest (how to multiply two numbers);
...a change in circumstances (two separate numbers are resolved into one expression);
...a sense of time ('*First*, you took the four and multiplied it by three...');
...a sense of place ('You put the one *under* the line...');

The response is always in narrative terms. If something as abstract as describing the solution of a mathematical problem displays the same narrative features as a fairy tale, it is a simple step to seeing that as humans we make sense of the world through narrative, through story.

As teachers, we enter the classroom already equipped as storytellers and the skills needed to transform the everyday storyteller into the teller of tales are neither mysterious nor arcane; they are simply a heightened and deliberate variation of those employed in the telling of stories in the staff room or pub. First among these skills, is the ability to identify and organise a clear narrative structure.

In my own work I have taken to using a simple rendering of the Actantial Analysis of the French semiotician, A. J. Greimas. At this point, I have known my undergraduate students to go slightly cross-eyed; however, the idea is a simple one and helps to make storytelling coherent and memorable. Sitting on the shoulders of Vladimir Propp (and his classification of Russian folk tales), Greimas draws us to consider not individual character types (such as king, step-mother or child) but the functions that the characters serve in the story. Greimas[2] identified six narrative functions:

1 *Subject*: the character around whom the narrative turns.
2 *Object*: that which the subject wants to achieve or acquire.
3 *Sender*: the person(s) or force(s) that moves the Subject to seek the Object.
4 *Receiver*: the person who benefits from the Subject's successful quest for the Object.
5 *Helper*: the person or force that aids the Subject in their quest for the Object.
6 *Opponent*: the person or force that opposes the Subject's completion of their quest for the Object.

These form binary pairs:

● Subject and Object
● Sender and Receiver
● Helper and Opponent.

And are usually arranged as:

$$\text{Sender} \longrightarrow \text{Object} \longleftarrow \text{Receiver}$$
$$\uparrow$$
$$\text{Helper} \longrightarrow \text{Subject} \longleftarrow \text{Opponent}$$

While a work of literature may generate a complex diagram (with more than one Subject, a series of Opponents and layers of Objects), it is possible to reduce folk tales (and other stories suitable for classroom use) to the simple binary pairs. Taking the example of 'Little Red Riding Hood' (as told by the Brothers Grimm), it would look like Figure 5.1.

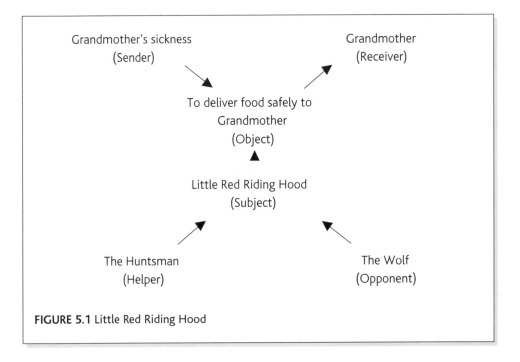

FIGURE 5.1 Little Red Riding Hood

If, as I suppose, we accept that as humans we understand ourselves and our world in narrative terms, and that simple narratives can be reduced to the functions of Subject, Object, Sender, Receiver, Helper and Opponent, then there is a clear implication for general teaching and specifically for creating narratives that assist children to become effective listeners and speakers. In our own teaching, we should be constructing narratives where these functions are clearly differentiated and assisting our students to do the same – and not just in specific times set aside for storytelling.

The application of storytelling technique applied to general teaching can be illustrated by taking the example of the Norman Conquest. In order to understand the story we could consider the functions that operate in the historical narrative for the opposing leaders. Placing William as the Subject, we can draw Figure 5.2.

I am not suggesting that Figure 5.2 provides a sufficient study of the Conquest, nor that students should be taught to make schematic diagrams of actantial function at Key Stage 2, but in trying to make sense of the story, this analysis

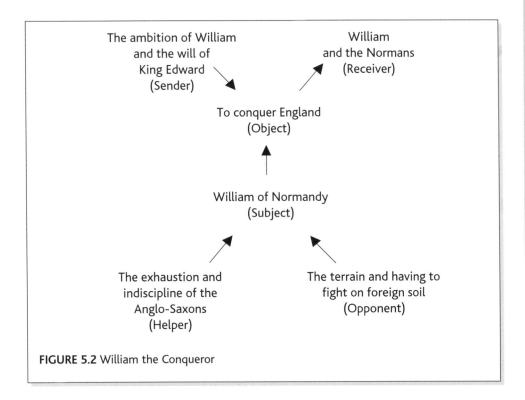

FIGURE 5.2 William the Conqueror

helps us to identify the key elements that create a coherent narrative from the history. Take one of these elements away, and the narrative is incomplete and fails to make sense. Hence by concentrating on narrative teaching, we are simply connecting with the way in which we naturally deal with information.

Returning to the teaching of multiplication it is even possible to identify the six functions of narrative, see Figure 5.3.

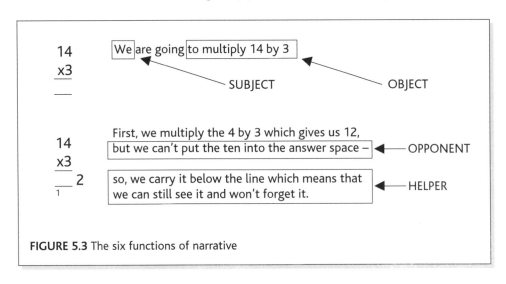

FIGURE 5.3 The six functions of narrative

Without any overt explanation the children will understand that the teacher is the Sender who initiates the activity, but the Receiver is still to be identified. A simple introduction that explains that this revisit to multiplication is to remind everyone of the methodology before going on to more complex problems implies that the pupils are the Receivers of the benefit of the activity.

Thus, an actantial approach not only provides a useful model for unfolding memorable and comprehensible tales in dedicated times of storytelling, but also hones our communication skills in all areas of the curriculum. In relating this approach to developing pupils' storytelling skills I often use sets of cards of archetypal characters (king, princess, child, etc.) places (castle, forest, desert, etc.) and situations (something lost, a curse, etc.), that groups or individuals can draw at random, and from which they then construct a simple narrative that can be told, acted out or represented in another way. For example, a 'WHO' card can provide the main character (the Subject), another is drawn to give a character trying to stop that protagonist (the Opponent) and another to be the person who provides help (the Helper). The protagonist's objective (the Object) can be generated by a 'WHERE' card (setting providing a context for the story and its destination) or a 'WHAT' card (mirror, sword, magic lamp, etc.). The missing elements of the Sender and Receiver can be drawn out of the children's ideas, and identified as the motivational force behind the action. Students have responded with great enthusiasm to activities such as these – developing their understanding of narrative framework in a playful atmosphere.

Narrative and memorisation

With no written text to rely on, you are dependent on your ability to memorise a story. The representation of a coherent narrative is key, not only to the comprehension of the children, but also to the memorisation of the story by the teacher.

Various writers on the craft of storytelling have suggested methods for memorising stories that have included creating a mental storyboard of images that can be linked together, drawing a 'spider diagram' of the major characters showing their relationships or writing a three line précis of the tale. While I have often used simple flow charts in order to remember strongly sequential narratives (such as creation myths), I have found that the actantial analysis outlined above is the most effective method of setting a story in my head in such a way that it has internal coherence when I tell it. Instead of trying to remember a list of events, I simply have to remember the motivating and opposing forces that come to play on the protagonist as they pursues their quest.

The basic rule is to use whatever method works for you with one proviso: do not learn a story word-for-word. Not only does this restrict the flexibility in the telling, it makes errors easier to make and harder to recover from. As the actantial method does not by necessity use phrasing drawn from a written text and depends on a more imaginative approach, it allows a freer flow of ideas.

Above all, the busy teacher needs to find ways in which to memorise stories that suit their personality as well as the available time. Once the story is learned it becomes incorporated into the teller's personal repertoire and can be told and retold – remembering that the story should change with every telling as the hearers change for as each group of children is unique, so is each storytelling event.

The selection of suitable material

I would love to be able to say that I learned this or that story sitting at the feet of an old woman as she unfolded the traditions of her people to her gathered family, but sadly I am dependent on my collection of story books (picked up on travels, yes, but rarely found at the feet of the elderly). Of course, stories can be, and are, drawn from all manner of sources and so in this section we will be looking at the way in which we, as busy professional people, can identify stories suitable for classroom use and to begin the process of adaptation.

Jack Zipes[3] writes:

> The best storytellers are thieves and forgers. They steal their tales from everywhere – books, television, films, radio, the Internet, and even other living human beings… Storytellers appropriate their stolen goods, make them their property, and re-present them as if the goods were their own material, which, in many ways, they are because storytellers always forge the tales they steal anew.

I regularly use one tale that has stayed with me since childhood. 'The Dog Gellert' was told to me as a small boy by my mother as I stood sobbing (always a sensitive child) next to the grave of the faithful hound slain in error by his master. The fact that I now know that both the tale and the grave are a romantic fiction has made no difference to the power of that narrative learned so many years ago; whatever the origins of the tale, the reason that I tell it is the emotional resonance it has for me as a childhood memory. This may seem a strange reason for choosing the story for classroom use, but it is vital that the teller has a real sympathy for the tales that s/he tells.

According to Teresa Grainger:[4]

> The importance of finding short tales which have an instinctive and immediate appeal should not be underestimated…Finding tales that are waiting to be told, that the storyteller really wants to share, for whatever conscious or unconscious reason, remains important. The hunt is not a quick or easy one, but it is always worth the journey.

Grainger's phrase 'tales that are waiting to be told' is extremely felicitous and it is certainly the feeling I have when I come across a story that I would like to use. For me, 'The Dog Gellert' is a tale waiting to be told.

There is a wealth of material to which the storyteller has access and with the advent of the worldwide web, the choice of tales is bewildering – giving some indication of the problem presented in selecting stories that are appropriate to the needs of the specific group of pupils. The first step, then, is to find a story which has a personal resonance from the moment that it is encountered, through adaptation, to the point where it is unfolded with the children.

Selection criteria

In addition to personal resonance I would suggest that a tale should fulfil the following criteria. Stories suitable for classroom use should have:

- *A coherent narrative*: Once we have an awareness of how coherent narrative is understood (in my methodology through the use of the Actantial Schema) we can identify stories that are both suitable for classroom use and easy to learn.

- *Linguistic comprehensibility*: The telling will need to be comprehensible to the children. However, this does not mean that the language of the source text needs to be at the appropriate level, for the language of delivery is dependent on you as storyteller rather than the original text.

- *An appropriateness to the developmental level of the students*: There is a huge differential between the developmental levels of students between Foundation Years and Year 6. The story should be appropriate to the emotional and social development of the students.

- *Cultural relevance*: It is essential to be aware of the culture within which you are working and its assumptions. For instance, in the Grimms' story of 'The Fisherman and His Wife' the shrewish wife wishes in turn for a house, a castle and a palace. Realising that she can't live in a palace as the wife of a fisherman, she wishes first to be the king, then emperor and then pope. In my telling I have edited the papacy from the story on the grounds that few children outside of Catholic families and schools would understand the role of the pope, or why his status is elevated above that of king and emperor. It could be argued that this story presents an opportunity to inform students about the place of the papacy in European culture. However, the reference to the pope appears immediately before the climax of the story when the wife wishes to be God; to interrupt the narrative in order to make an historical point would destroy the narrative flow and the sense of progressive tension.

Story may be also be a means of valuing the various ethnic cultures present in the classroom setting and building a bridge by which pupils can negotiate their way between the dominant host and minority cultures; all cultures have their own histories, myths, legends and stories which are passed on through generations of children. These stories cross cultural boundaries; some are recognisably similar with subtle shades of difference, others will be particular within a specific cultural context. In either case the story itself becomes a powerful shared experience.[5]

Experience of working as a storyteller in multicultural schools where there are ethnic tensions has informed my own practice. The response of students from Turkish families in some inner-city schools in Belgium to a simple folk tale from Turkey has shown me what an affirming effect simple storytelling can have. That the non-Turkish students are also engaged with an amusing tale that anyone would be hard-pressed to dislike is an important consideration, given the tensions between groups of students from different ethnic backgrounds in some of Belgium's schools.

- *A curriculum link*: The story may be a means of supporting curriculum studies, or introducing themes. For instance, if in science you were looking at the solar system, you could use a story such as the Native American myth 'How Grandmother Spider Stole the Sun'[6] to explore the ways in which different peoples have tried to explain what they see in the night sky.

- *A socially constructive message*: While I don't want to enter a debate on the rights and wrongs of story as social manipulation within the education system, it has to be acknowledged that classroom storytelling exists within the school context and cannot escape being part of the structured environment of learning for the child. In addition to being a primary agent for constructing future society, every teacher faces social issues within the classroom itself, from bullying, to bereavement to the effects of family breakdown, among their students. Although we should beware of seeing storytelling as a panacea for the ills of society, the told tale can be a powerful tool in speaking for the marginalised and the bolstering the cause of social justice within the school community.

Finding suitable stories

Faced with the array of possible sources for classroom storytelling, I would suggest the following process, which reduces the amount of time that is wasted:

1 First, make your choice of story collection. This may be made because of the need to support the curriculum, or to find something with a specific cultural

relevance or socially constructive message. I tend to avoid most children's versions of story books; when I am looking for a story that appeals to me, I am seeking something that expresses itself in language with which I am comfortable. When I retell the story to young people I tell my own version and the language is then tailored to their needs. (Please note, however, I am not beyond cross-checking with children's versions to see how others have adapted tales.)

2   Scan the contents or the index and see if there is a title or reference that catches your attention.

3   Speed read the first and last paragraph (or two) of a few stories. This should enable you to identify the main protagonist and the theme.

4   Read through any story that seems to arrest your attention more than the others, but do not be afraid to reject them based on the criteria and try reading the next story and so on.

The adaptation of the story

Once you have found a story that is *waiting to be told*, the next question is whether it has a *simple coherent narrative* (or is adaptable to one). In other words, whether it is possible to easily identify the Subject, Object, Sender, Receiver, Helper and Opponent.

Once the structural elements have been identified, the tale needs adapting to the particular group to whom you are going to be telling. I wouldn't want to say that *linguistic comprehensibility* will look after itself, but language is something that will change with each telling of the story. Although you should avoid writing the story out word-for-word as you intend to tell it, you may wish to think about particular opportunities for the use of rhythm, rhyme, alliterative phrasing, onomatopoeia and imagery (and the original text may act as a source here).

As with all teaching materials you will need to exercise professional judgement with regard to the *appropriateness to the developmental level of the students* of the tale. If the main theme of a story is the protagonist's Oedipal desires then it is probably not going to be suitable for Key Stages 1 or 2 as it stands. However, you should not fear making adjustments to create a coherent narrative that is targeted at your particular group of children.

Cultural relevance is extremely important. In an exercise for undergraduates on the adaptation of traditional tales to classroom use it may appropriate to use the Grimms' tale 'Hans My Hedgehog' in full – including the hero washing his black skin until it is white. However, in the classroom there would need to be considerable editing to make the story useable.[7] Hence, as with 'The Fisherman and His Wife', if on a close reading a story has elements which are inaccessible, there is no problem with judicious cutting; the key point is that this is a personal telling of a traditional tale.

It is vital to realise that few children have had no exposure to traditional stories in some form and there will often be a very strong sense of ownership of a particular version. When I first started as a storyteller I was often faced with children who would correct me ('No, that's wrong, the shoe was made of glass'). A solution presented itself at a seminar led by the storyteller Sandra Pollerman who informed the group that she always finished her stories with the phrase:

That was the story of _____, and that was how I told it.

and I have used the formula since. This simple phrase allows one to claim ownership of the tale and justifies deviating from the commonly received form of a story (often, sadly, courtesy of the Disney Corporation). In fact I often modify the formula to:

That was the story of _____, and that was how you and I told it.

The *curriculum link* can be established where it desirable or necessary and *a socially constructive message* may be sought (avoiding any temptation to sermonise).

Bowdlerisation – a word about a word

Related to the adaptation and editing of stories is the issue of *bowdlerisation* (after Thomas Bowdler (1754–1825) who published an expurgated edition of Shakespeare). The fear of violence and sexuality has led to what might be referred to as the Disneyfication, first, of European folk tradition and now that of other cultures.

Although some blame may be laid at the door of the 'Magic Kingdom', Disney has simply been the most successful of many forces promoting a romantic notion of childhood and society which has little relevance to the world as children experience it – nor indeed to the world of traditional stories. We like to forget that Cinderella's ugly sisters had their eyes pecked out, that Snow White's step-mother danced to her death in red-hot shoes and that Manypelts was sought in marriage by her own father.

Bruno Bettelheim[8] (most famously) suggests that children have monsters, violence and desires deep inside their subconscious. The role of the folk tale has been to give an imaginative language to that violence and to place the monsters and desires in a context that serves society's structures.

Adults often think that the cruel punishment of an evil person in fairy tales upsets and scares children unnecessarily. Quite the opposite is true: such retribution reassures the child that the punishment fits the crime. The child often feels unjustly treated by adults and the world in general, and it seems that nothing is done about it... the more severely those bad ones are dealt with, the more secure the child feels.

In the traditional versions of 'Snow White' and 'Cinderella' there is clear retribution for the wrongs done to the girls – retributive justice that will accord with the moral level of children at KS1 and 2. In the same way these stories reinforce taboos in a symbolic form which although it may be inappropriate to examine explicitly, work on a subconscious level (e.g. Manypelts and her father's incestuous intentions, Little Red Riding Hood climbing into bed with the (older male) Wolf).

It is possible that the lack of a truly enriched inner life may lead to frustration which manifests itself as violence. We must, therefore, think hard before trimming the extremes from traditional tales to make them more acceptable or politically correct. From my own experience as a teacher of children with profound emotional and behavioural difficulties, I would support the view that the child needs an imaginative capacity for violence in order to express their anger, but it must be made clear, however, that this argument does not justify allowing the young access to violent films or images. These do not provide an imaginative vocabulary or stimulate the imagination to creativity; visual representations of violence force the imagination into a particular predetermined form which the shared story doesn't. Obviously sensitivity is required. Too much detail of violence and you are again forcing the child into seeing images that may be inappropriate or frightening; too little, and the child fails to find a world where right is rewarded and evil pays the price of its crimes.[9]

Absence and completion – engagement and story

The longer that I practise as a storyteller, the more convinced I become that the key to good storytelling – the key to good teaching – is the principle of *absence and completion.*

The word 'absence' can be used in many contexts, not all of them positive: absence of listeners, absence of attention, absence of understanding, absence of humour. But all of these would be despite the teacher and the storyteller. When I speak of 'absence' I am specifically referring to moments where an element of the narrative is missing and has to be provided by the hearers. This absence is controlled by the storyteller and is intentional and contrived. Aimed at stimulating the imagination of the students, crafted moments of absence point that imagination along a particular path or paths without constricting it.

In this sense, absence may be manifest in a missing word or phrase that the students have to provide:

Storyteller:	But Siput the snail kept on walking,
	he kept on walking,
	he kept on ...

| Students: | ...walking! |

It may be in supplying information needed to complete the story:

| Storyteller: | The first animal to knock on the witch's door was the...the... |
| | You know, I've forgotten; what animal do you think it was? |

It could be visual absence where a person, place or object is 'seen' by the storyteller in what is empty space, but an empty space that is filled by the imaginations of the children.

Storyteller:	[cupping hands and focusing eyes on the space between
	them]...and the Lord God looked down at the body of the dead
	swallow and said to the angels, 'You have chosen well...'

or, the absence could be one of additional significance where an everyday object gains a new meaning through the way it is used in the storytelling:

Storyteller:	The fisherman rowed his little boat out into the blue sea... [the
	storyteller takes a long piece of blue cloth and creates ripples
	in it to signify water]

With moments of visual absence, the imagination is engaged in bridging the gap between reality and the textual reference (between blue fabric and the sea). It also anchors the whole group to a specific object or space, creating a shared moment of recognition and transformation.

One of the main differences between the story that is read and the tale that is told is the breadth of opportunities that the latter presents for creating moments of absence, engaging the hearers and make them participators rather than passive hearers. It is sadly the case that many performance activities (whether storytelling, acting, dancing or singing) would be identical whether or not an audience was present. This is not to recommend an 'it's behind you!' approach to every mode of performance, but it is possible for the audience to affect the piece of work. In fact, I would echo the director Peter Brook[10] who rejects the activity of 'watching' a play because of its suggestion of passivity, preferring the French word 'assistance', which has connotations of contribution to the event:

In the French language amongst the different terms for those who watch, for public, for spectator, one word stands out, is different in quality from the rest. *Assistance* – I watch a play: *j'assiste à une pièce*. To assist – the word is simple: it is the key.

By creating moments of absence and completion, the storyteller assures the students that their listening is valued and at the same time the children know that the story cannot continue without them. When the pupils are asked to contribute to the story and their assistance is incorporated into the narrative, they see that what they bring to the story as integral to the telling and part of the continuous whole.

Some final thoughts

My formative experiences as a storyteller were from working with children with emotional and behavioural difficulties. Such students often experience problems with imaginative play and I found that closing the book and telling rather than reading a story had a dramatic effect on their ability to maintain attention and respond – to the point that I was sometimes able to use storytelling techniques to calm distressed and hysterical pupils.

At this point I need to counsel against using storytelling to practise quasi-psychological therapies. One of the features of contemporary storytelling is its association with various forms of spirituality and mysticism and there are those who wish to 'give prescriptions for self-healing through stories' (Mellon 1992). While such aims may be laudable, they presume a clinical expertise that few teachers possess and what is more, distance storytelling from the prosaic day-to-day existence of classroom teaching. Storytelling in the classroom will not mould either emotional or cognitive development of children, but it is a powerful technique that can be utilised to great effect as an element of a complete education.

To provide a meaningful experience of storytelling, whether teaching the physical properties of material science or telling the tale of Little Red Riding Hood, the same rules apply:

- a clear coherent narrative that is unmediated by a written text;
- the use of material that is appropriate to the developmental level of the children and the cultural context in which they exist;
- the controlled and varied use of absence and completion that engages the children in the storytelling event.

Every time that I teach storytelling I find myself repeating the mantra 'you are already storytellers'; in the pub, round the table in the staff room we all tell stories to our families, our friends and our colleagues. The teacher who wishes to be an effective teller of tales in his/her class simply has to refine those storytelling skills they put to use every day.

In regaling friends with the latest disaster in our relationship with the school's photocopier we will use all the elements that have been identified in this chapter:

we will select the story, identify the elements of narrative and adapt it to our audience; we will even engage in absence and completion miming the prodding of the green start button and asking 'Go on, guess what happened next!'

Although I may be depriving myself of work, I hope that I have provided ample reason for every teacher to see themselves as (at the very least) a nascent storyteller.

Notes

1. DfES (2003).
2. Greimas and Cortes (1982).
3. Zipes (2004).
4. Grainger (1997).
5. Wyse and Jones (2001).
6. See Bruchac (1991).
7. In fact, I do use a version of 'Hans my Hedgehog' as it presents a male hero who is vulnerable and unwanted – a role often reserved for girls in popular story collections.
8. See Bettelheim (1991).
9. The irony in British culture is a counter-movement that led to the removal of a story of theft, wife battery, child abuse and murder, from the public houses where it had previously been told and its assimilation into the culture of childhood. If you doubt that such a thing is possible, then I would suggest a stroll along the beach at Eastbourne (or any of a number of seaside towns) this summer, and take an informative break watching a Punch and Judy show.
10. See Brook (1972).

References and further reading

Bettelheim, B. (1991) *The Uses of Enchantment.* London: Penguin Books.

Brook, P. (1972) *The Empty Space.* London: Penguin.

Bruchac, J. (1991) *Native American Stories.* Golden, CO: Fulcrum Publishing.

DfES (2003) *Speaking, Listening, Learning: Working with Children in Key Stages 1 and 2.* London: DfES.

Egan, K. (1989) *Teaching as Story Telling.* Chicago, IL: University of Chicago Press.

Grainger, T. (1997) *Traditional Storytelling in the Primary Classroom.* Leamington Spa: Scholastic.

Greimas, A.J. and Cortes, J. (1982) *Semiotics and Language. An Analytical Dictionary* (trans. L. Crist *et al.*). Bloomington, IN: Indiana University Press.

Grugeon, E. and Gardner, P. (2000) *The Art of Storytelling for Teachers and Pupils.* London: David Fulton Publishers.

Mellon, N. (1992) *The Art of Storytelling.* Shaftesbury: Element Books.

Wyse, D. and Jones, R. (2001) *Teaching English, Language and Literacy.* London: RoutledgeFalmer.

Zipes, J. (1995) *Creative Storytelling.* London: Routledge.

Zipes, J. (2004) *Speaking Out, Storytelling and Creative Drama for Children.* London: Routledge.

Letting talents shine: developing oracy with gifted and talented pupils

Mary Williams

Introduction

In this chapter, the role of speaking and listening, as it relates to gifted and talented children – across the Foundation Stage and Key Stages 1 and 2 – will be explored, drawing on findings from a DfES Key Stage 1 Gifted and Talented project – 'Nurturing Young Talent' (NYT), which has been running for the past three years.[1] Oracy is at the heart of learning and occurs in most subjects of the curriculum in some form or another, although it develops initially as young children learn through play. Therefore, consideration will be given to the teacher's role in supporting the speaking and listening of gifted and talented pupils in both the Literacy Hour and while teaching other subjects of the National Curriculum (1999).

All children – especially higher ability pupils – need to be motivated through challenging activities that involve them in deep levels of thinking and discussion with others during whole-class or group activities across the primary school curriculum. On an individual level, they need to be aware that they use 'inner speech' as the medium in which to think. As part of reflection on learning, opportunities for pupils to gain metacognitive awareness need to be given, as this offers yet another important dimension to thinking, i.e. by getting them to think about *how* they have learned something, as well as to share *what* they have discovered in the course of any investigation.

In terms of literacy, oracy underpins learning to read and write. Therefore, the inter-relationship of speaking and listening to reading and writing will be examined to show how the precocious oral abilities that many gifted and talented children possess can be utilised to the full. The need for some of these pupils to be given a listening agenda will also be explored. Practical ways to challenge higher ability pupils will be suggested, in particular, through the use of 'dialogue and questioning', 'discussion', 'presentation' and 'drama' across the Programmes of Study of the English Curriculum – speaking and listening, writing and reading. The premise that creative, problem-solving tasks are vital if gifted and talented children are to remain focused and to learn effectively will provide the backdrop to the debate.

The rights of gifted and talented pupils

However, to put the discussion into perspective, the rights of gifted and talented children need some consideration. Until the setting up of the Gifted and Talented unit at the DfES five years ago, the educational needs of higher ability pupils had not been a high priority in the UK. For example, as recently as 2002 in Ofsted's evaluation of the National Literacy Strategy little reference was made to whether they were being catered for appropriately.

Gifts and talents, whatever they may be, need nurturing, as they are unlikely to develop on their own. All children should be given a curriculum that provides them with the 'optimal match' (CTY 1994) with their learning potential and nowhere is this more important than for gifted and talented pupils. This match will be achieved when an appropriately challenging curriculum is adjusted to match the child's pace and level of learning. Higher ability children have the right to a stimulating, challenging and creative education; something that is of vital importance if early potential is to flourish.

Consequently, they require a differentiated curriculum that will meet their needs along with those of the rest of the ability spectrum in the class. This is not always easy to achieve, particularly in classrooms where there is a wide range of ability. To leave higher ability pupils to take care of themselves is risky because, as most teachers would agree, idle, unchallenged minds will soon find alternative, and sometimes inappropriate, ways of keeping amused. Reassuringly, however, gifted and talented do not require a curriculum that is radically different from other pupils in the class but one in which the pace is faster and level of instruction deeper and where the accent is on them reflecting about what they are doing. According to the QCA (2001), there are five crucial dimensions to the work they should be given:

- breadth
- depth
- acceleration
- independence
- time for reflection.

Teachers can set all the children in a class the same task but with different, more challenging outcomes being required from higher ability pupils. Activities should be planned so that they become progressively more difficult as pupils work through them, based on the assumption that the more able will reach these quicker. Sometimes higher ability pupils can be set different tasks from the rest of the class, specifically geared to their own interests to provide them with essential motivation for learning, such as when they are supported in finding out more about a personal interest.

In conclusion, therefore, to make the most of their education gifted and talented pupils should be given tasks that demand high levels of commitment from them through an enriched curriculum (Renzulli 1994) that captures their imaginations and nurtures their potential. This will be achieved via creative, problem-solving tasks that sometimes involve collaboration with peers (good for their sociability) that often require an oral outcome. Ways of developing such a curriculum for gifted and talented pupils will now be looked at in more depth.

Thinking across the curriculum

All children need to be given time to think and to express their ideas across a range of curriculum subjects. They need to know how to discuss ways to solve problems in creative and systematic ways. They need to be able to outline their findings so that they are accessible to other children in the class, as well as to pupils of similar ability to themselves. This is unlikely to be achieved without direct input or modelling by teachers about how best to undertake these activities. One of the problems with oracy teaching – or the lack of it – in the past has been that it was assumed that as talking comes naturally to most people, it could be left to its own devices. Equally, although often orally adept, gifted and talented pupils may need help to become active and sympathetic listeners. This is essential if they are to become socially confident, as well as intellectually able. To be successful across subjects of the primary curriculum children need to be encouraged to think about what they are learning and how they are learning it. This will best be achieved while carrying out stimulating, creative tasks.

Encouraging gifted and talented children to think

The important relationship between 'speaking and listening' and thinking has been acknowledged for a long time.[2] Gifted and talented pupils, in particular, need the match and pace of the curriculum to be accelerated and deepened (as above). This can be gained through challenging them to higher levels of thinking through motivating them to solve interesting and relevant problems. To achieve this teachers need to ask questions that require reflective and elaborated responses (Fisher 2001): higher order thinking that comes near to the top of Bloom's taxonomy (1956) involving:

- analysis;
- synthesis;
- evaluation.

(Koshy and Casey 1997)

High levels of thinking like this occur when children generate outcomes that show imagination and originality and are capable of being thoughtfully evaluated. Essential to this is a questioning classroom, where teachers and pupils ask unusual and challenging questions; where new connections are made; where ideas are represented in different ways – visually, physically and verbally – and where innovative approaches to finding solutions are encouraged. Through such lessons children develop new thinking as they generate and extend ideas in collaboration with each other and their teachers. To assess whether a particular lesson has stimulated the children to think creatively look for evidence of pupils doing the following:

- applying their imagination;
- generating their own questions, hypotheses, ideas and outcomes;
- developing skills or techniques through creative activity;
- using judgement to assess their own or others' creative work.

(Fisher and Williams 2004)

Encouraging gifted and talented children to be creative

There are several keys to unlocking creativity.[3] Most of these are speech dependent; be it through actual discussion with others or via 'inner speech' as pupils reflect upon what they are doing. These keys include:

- motivation;
- inspiration;
- gestation;
- collaboration.

(Fisher and Williams 2004)

Creativity is a critical element in fostering ability. It takes children beyond the here and now into realms of thinking that involve using the imagination to solve problems that transcend curriculum subjects. Being creative depends on the use of multiple intelligences (Gardner 1993), with one of these being 'linguistic'. Therefore, children need stimulating problem-solving tasks to encourage them to think creatively.

With young children this can often be achieved through play. In the *Curriculum Guidance for the Foundation Stage* (DfEE 2000a) play is seen as both a context for children's learning and a means of keeping motivation alive. In the UK the Foundation Stage (for children from the ages of three to five years) and Key Stage 1 (from five to seven years) is where the potential of play as a means of learning about the world and each other can be maximised. It is counter-productive to start formal learning too soon because children learn best in ways that are holistic and context-specific. Learning through play is beneficial because, at the time, the play activity is the child's world with a reality of its own, but to have purpose it needs to be carefully planned. Here is an example of an activity devised for Key Stage 1 Gifted and Talented children.

In this example from the NYT project, 2004, in a school in the London Borough of Hounslow the children were asked to solve the following problem – how can you transfer water from one water tray to another using a variety of pipes and containers? (The trays were too far apart for water to be tipped straight from one to the other.) The children selected for this activity had already shown an ability to be experimental and to take risks in a previous water-based activity. A large percentage of children in this school were using English as an additional language (EAL) so it was decided to set up the task using a mixture of gesture and simple verbal interaction. Throughout the task the children found ways of communicating with one another, providing a useful platform on which social interaction and oral confidence could grow. Above all, they revealed spatial and interpersonal intelligence in interpreting the task as well as emergent scientific concepts about water (Figure 6.1).

Once completed, the activity was reviewed by the staff involved and the following conclusions were reached. Tasks for higher ability EAL learners need to be:

- culturally accessible to all;
- related to previous experience;
- child-centred;
- not too language-dependent;
- large-scale and motivating to appeal to all genders;
- open-ended – lasting for more than one session with children being given as much time as they need to complete them;
- resourced easily with overnight storage being considered from the outset.

To make sure that play is purposeful, as in the example above, it must be challenging, so that all children, but particularly those who are gifted and talented, are encouraged to think deeply and learn to persevere while engaging in imaginative and interesting activities. They can be encouraged to explore new objects or ideas if asked to think about them in terms of the following:

FIGURE 6.1 'We are proud of what we've done'

- Does it (object, artefact or photograph) remind you of anything?
- Have you done anything like this yourself before?
- What does it smell (taste, feel, look or sound) like?

Their imaginations need to be fostered as they are asked probing questions with language being used increasingly to mediate understanding, for example, when adults respond to what children are doing and/or saying by asking these sorts of questions:

- Do you mean that...?
- I think I understand what you are saying. You think that...?
- What would happen if...?
- What else do you need to think about?
- Is there another way of doing that?
- How does that help?

(Williams, in Fisher and Williams 2004)

Adults have sometimes been reluctant to intervene in children's play because they are afraid that they will disrupt the imaginative flow, but high levels of interaction involving questioning, the recall and reformulation of ideas by the child, will deepen its quality. Therefore, through high levels of questioning gifted and talented children can be encouraged to think deeply by being asked to evaluate what did or did not work.

The role of the teacher

The role of the teacher will be critical in developing children's 'gifts and talents'. It will involve them in planning an appropriately differentiated curriculum and in asking searching questions (as above). In particular, they will need to be aware of the important role that 'speaking and listening' plays in education, for example, in:

- identifying gifts and talents;
- teaching gifted and talented pupils a variety of learning techniques;
- knowing how to give gifted and talented pupils metacognitive awareness.

Identifying gifts and talents

Problems about how to identify gifted and talented pupils still remain; one reason for the setting up of the DfES Gifted and Talented unit. Characteristics established from research undertaken in Kent suggest that oral ability has a large part to play in this as can be seen in many of the attributes listed:

- is continuously demanding;
- is very curious;
- possesses a vivid imagination;
- learns more quickly than other children;
- has a good memory;
- has great physical energy;
- can concentrate for long periods if interested;
- begins to speak and read earlier than chronological peers;
- has a wide vocabulary;
- pays great attention to detail;
- has a well-developed sense regarding social matters, e.g. leadership, taking turns, self-awareness, nuances in interaction, 'tunes in' to what is going on;

- frequently asks questions, sometimes speculative or philosophical in nature;
- shows a sense of humour that may be unusual or odd;
- challenges by asking 'why'.

(Baczala 2003)[4]

Teaching gifted and talented pupils a variety of learning techniques

There are various ways that gifted and talented children can be challenged through speaking and listening learning techniques. These include:

- challenging dialogues and probing questioning;
- presenting;
- drama;
- providing a listening agenda;
- working in a group.

Challenging dialogues and probing questioning

Learning occurs most successfully when gifted and talented children engage in challenging dialogues with adults (and each other) as part of solving problems or investigating new objects or ideas. As a means of getting pupils of higher ability to be creative in their thinking they need to be provided with cognitive challenges that often involve them in working with each other towards specific, motivating goals as in the water play challenge above. Tasks that offer this should include information processing and questioning as part of challenging dialogues between children and their teachers.

The adult's role in such dialogues is to ask probing questions that do the following:

- make challenging cognitive demands of the child;
- manage the response – by providing models of how to synthesise disparate items of learning;
- help the child to see a task/problem through sequentially;
- help the child to select appropriate materials to solve the problem set;
- check that the child's response is appropriate;
- keep the child *actively* involved;
- pace questions asked, so that the number of probing questions asked keeps up the momentum;

- give shape to a session – by drawing the threads of learning and understanding together in a plenary and inviting children to do this for themselves.

(adapted from Meadows and Cashdan 1988, and Fisher and Williams 2004)

In this activity from an 'Upside Down Day' project undertaken as part of a small schools NYT project in Dorset in 2004, the whole class (five- and six-year-olds) were introduced at first to the idea through a drama activity that centred on them waking up to find that everything was upside down to what it normally was. The discussion that this engendered was highly dependent on a challenging dialogue between pupils and teacher. Also, as this activity was to be shared among four schools, ideas for it were set out clearly in the accompanying documentation, including suggestions for a series of probing questions that included the following:

- What made you think about ... ?
- How do you ... ?
- What were you thinking when ... ?
- How would your life be different?
- Think of something that would be a problem?
- How would you solve it?

The children were asked to record their thoughts in speech or thought bubbles that were entered on 'mind maps' relating to the central themes that had emerged in the initial dialogue, e.g. it is dark not light, people are walking in the sky, you have lunch before breakfast, etc. Gifted and talented children were identified by the 'special' insight they showed, for example, one child wrote about it snowing in summer, a mouse chasing a cat and the sea being yellow and the sand blue, while another attempted to write words backwards.

Presenting

Sometimes higher ability pupils can be asked to present findings from work across the curriculum, either individually, in pairs or as a group. Preparation for presentations will be needed so that pupils are analytical and systematic in their thinking, as they decide what to include, what to leave out and the order in which various points should be introduced. A proforma could be prepared like the one below to assist this process.

Preparing a presentation

Ask yourself these questions and note down the answers so that they can be shared with others:

- What do I already know about the subject?
- Why am I interested in it?
- What else do I want to know?
- How and where will I find this out?
- What questions are still unanswered or have arisen during my investigation?
- Does anyone in the audience know the answers to any of these?
- Does anyone want to ask any questions?

Using artefacts or pictures to make the presentation more interesting should be considered as well as PowerPoint so that source material from the internet can be easily included.

Drama

Another way of getting higher ability pupils to share their knowledge is through the use of the drama technique of 'hot-seating'. (This was used in 'The Upside Down Day' project (above) so that children could share their ideas before attempting to write them down and during which they were challenged to justify their opinions by their teacher and other children.) Gifted and talented children can also take on 'the mantle of the expert' for a particular subject or focus and can be questioned about what they know about it by other children in the class (Johnson, in Fisher and Williams 2006). They are the ones in the know and the challenge is for them to share what they have found out with others in an interesting and accessible way (see Chapter 7 for more details).

Providing a listening agenda

Gifted and talented children may need to be given a specific focus during some direct teaching inputs or discussions as they can be impatient and disruptive when not allowed to speak or answer first. A way to do this is to set them a 'listening' agenda and this also ensures that they do not hog the limelight all the time, as this can be very demotivating for other pupils in the class. It involves giving them something specific to listen for or a challenge that asks them to 'analyse, synthesis and evaluate' the contribution of others. To improve their powers of analysise this can take the form of summing up the evidence offered in a debate, or at the end of a discussion relating to an investigative piece of work, e.g. in Science or History.

A listening agenda could include the following:

- listening to a poem and being asked to discuss it on several levels – literal, figurative, emotional, inferential and deductive;

- assessing the motivation of a particular character from a story or poem that has been read out loud to the class;
- taking a passive role in a group as scribe or balancer (see below), including assessing whether the mode of address adopted by the speaker was appropriate to the task in hand;
- listening out for particular information in a presentation or during direct input on a subject by the teacher;
- listening to information given by another (or others), making notes about it and writing it up in the form of a newspaper article;
- listening to a persuasive speech or reading in order to comment on the features that made it effective or not;
- summing up on a particular theme/lesson as a result of findings offered by several children to assess whether a consensus has been reached or whether there is disparity between sources.[5]

Working in a group

By implication, much of the work suggested above will require gifted and talented children to collaborate with one another. This, in itself, can be quite a challenge for them, as they can be highly individualistic and easily irritated if others do not keep up with their pace of learning. Such work will only be effective if pupils know how to operate successfully in a group.

In addition to the subject-based, problem-solving nature of any task pupils need to understand how to work in a group (Williams 2000). Therefore, during any reporting back session, children need to evaluate the effectiveness of the discussion itself. To facilitate this they can be given roles within the group such as chair, scribe or *balancer*. This last role can be usefully given to higher ability children, as they have to listen very carefully to each contributor to report back whether certain individuals dominated the discussion in order to determine who took the lead, so increasing their understanding of group dynamics. This may have a salutary effect on them by making them aware of how it can feel to others when someone always hogs the limelight. The role of *scribe* could also be given to gifted and talented children who tend to take the automatic lead during discussions. This gives others a chance to speak and might make the scribe more sensitive to the needs of others in the class; all part of the process of socialisation. In these more passive roles they could be asked to decide whether those who speak the most actually make the greatest contribution to the discussion and should give evidence-based reasons for any conclusions they reach. In a more active way they could be in the *chair* as this would involve them in analysing and evaluating the contribution of others as they sum up what has been learned.

Finally, to ensure that gifted and talented are sensitive towards others when engaging in dialogues with them or when taking on the role of an expert they should be encouraged to use a 'praise sandwich' so that others in the class feel that their contributions have been valued, i.e. offer something positive on the top and bottom, with an area for growth or contention in the middle.

Knowing how to give gifted and talented pupils metacognitive awareness

Gifted and talented children should be given challenges on higher levels of thinking such as analysis, synthesis and evaluation (as above). This brings together thinking, questioning and dialogue skills as shown in Table 6.1.

Table 6.1 Thinking, questioning and dialogue skills

Thinking skills (NC)	Characteristic questions	Features of dialogue
Information-processing	What is it about?	Relevant information is shared
Reasoning	What does it mean?	Reasons are expected
Enquiry	What do we need to know?	Questions are asked
Creative thinking	Can we add to it?	Ideas are developed
Evaluation	What do we think about it?	Judgements are made

(Fisher and Williams 2002)

Through such high levels of thinking, gifted and talented children will be challenged to achieve at levels commensurate with their learning potential. Levels of thinking will be deepened even further if attention is paid to metacognition.

The term 'metacognition' was first used by Flavell in 1976 and refers to an individual's own awareness and consideration of his or her cognitive processes and strategies. It relates to the human capacity to be self-reflective, not just to think and know, but to think about how you think and know. Vygotsky (1962) argued that when the process of learning is brought to a conscious level, children become aware of their own thought processes and this helps them to gain control over the way they learn. It is not just about the integration of information with knowledge, but involves directing attention to what has been assimilated and understood, and the relationship of this, to the processes of learning itself.

Metacognition includes knowledge of self, as a thinker and learner, in relation to a task and in relation to a particular context. It develops the thinking ability of the learner as the levels of thinking become gradually deeper as implicit understanding becomes explicit. This works in the following way:

Levels of awareness

1 *Tacit use*: Children make decisions without really thinking about them.

2 *Aware use*: Children become consciously aware of a strategy or decision-making process.

3 *Strategic use*: Children are able to select the best strategies for solving a problem.

4 *Reflective use*: Children can reflect on their thinking, before, during and after the process and evaluate progress and set targets for improvement.

(Fisher and Williams 2002)

However, getting children to think about thinking is not easy; it is a complex teaching skill that depends on three key factors, i.e.:

- the task must be worthy of serious thought;
- the thinking and reasoning of pupils must be valued;
- time must be given for thinking about their thinking.

It can be made more accessible through 'modelling'. Teachers can help children to think metacognitively by modelling their own thinking processes as they engage in a range of tasks. After this, some higher ability pupils may be capable of 'modelling' themselves. This gives them an oral challenge, as they need to reveal their thinking processes to other children. If pupils are to be involved in this they will need to rehearse what they are going to say either with their teacher, or with each other if they are working in a group or as a pair. Asking oneself metacognitive questions will be useful in this respect (or these questions can be asked by the teacher). Metacognitive questions might include:

- How did you start to solve the problem?
- Did you go up any blind alleys?
- What was particularly useful in working it out?
- Did you consider any alternative ideas?
- Why did you reject these?
- How did you figure it out?
- Would you go about a similar task in the same way?

Significantly, metacognitive awareness gained in this way can help children to make conscious decisions about how to tackle similar learning tasks in the future (Williams 2000).

Speaking and listening and the Literacy Hour

Oral ability underpins learning to read and to write so it is a vital component of literacy learning. Little direct guidance was given on how to teach higher ability children in the National Literacy Strategy (1998) although some attempt to identify what gifted and talented pupils are able to do was offered later on. They are:

- able to orchestrate the various reading cues at an early age;
- *active readers* who can generalise from their reading experience.

And in writing they are able to do the following:

- latch on quickly to the conventions of different types of writing;
- *think in original ways and experiment with new styles*;
- manipulate language, sentence structure and punctuation;
- *use apt terminology and varied vocabulary.*

(DfEE 2000b)

Implicit in this are several references to 'speaking and listening' and thinking skills (in italics above) but it was not until the 'English National Curriculum' (1999) set out teaching objectives for 'speaking' and 'listening' separately (although the two are closely related), as well as for group discussion and interaction and discussion, that this was given true weight.[6]

It is important to make use of the 'precocious oral ability' that many higher ability children possess to help them become fully involved in the Literacy Hour. They need to be asked to justify the language choices, or the conclusions they have reached as part of shared, guided or independent work. They can share what they have earned in a particular lesson, or from an investigation, during the plenary session where they can be encouraged to 'think aloud' (see above) by telling others what they were thinking about as they went about a task. This gives less able pupils metacognitive understanding while providing a challenge for the more able as they have to put themselves across in a way that is accessible to others.

Speaking and listening and reading

Through problem-solving activities gifted and talented children can be challenged to demonstrate what they have understood from reading a range of texts in a variety of ways. They can be required to offer opinions about the personality and motivation of particular characters in novels. Giving children access to an idea by discussing how they think they would experience it, if it happened to them, can be stimulated by reading them carefully chosen extracts from stories and poems as part of text level work. Higher ability children need to be set challenges that captivate them on an emotional, as well as intellectual, level. They can respond to themes in stories by offering evidence-based reasons for their thoughts about the issues raised. This will take them deeper inside the author's thinking and help them when they start to write on similar themes for themselves. Discussion with a response partner will help to increase understanding as long as preparatory work on how to go about this is undertaken (see below).

Similarly, children can be asked to justify conclusions reached as a result of researching into a particular problem. This may take the form of an individual enquiry but may involve pupils in high levels of discussion with similar ability children, either in their own class during group work or perhaps by making links over the Internet with higher ability children from other schools. Findings can be shared with other pupils, possibly in a higher class or with others in their own (see above about preparing for a presentation). To provide appropriate depth and challenge through reading, more complex texts should be made available to gifted and talented children, who should be asked searching questions about them, for example:

- How do you know that?
- How did you learn that?
- What evidence do you have for that?
- Are there words in story that led you to think that?
- Can you think of another word that means the same as...?
- What do you think s/he meant by the words...?

Searching for information via the Internet can provide another reading challenge. Whatever the source, children need to be taught to discriminate between sources and to be aware of the possibility of bias.

Speaking and listening and writing

There are several ways this might occur including through:

- oral composition;
- writing conferences;
- being a response partner.

Oral composition

To encourage higher ability pupils to develop their writing teachers should help them understand the processes involved (Hodson and Jones 2001). Oral composition is a crucial part of the writing process and has been highlighted as an important factor in giving young children the confidence to write. It helps to avoid the blank page syndrome that puts so many off. One device to avoid this was used by an NYT project school in the London Borough of Richmond, based on an idea from *The Shape Game* by Anthony Browne. The teacher drew a number of non-representational shapes on a piece of paper and the gifted and talented children in the group were asked to say what they reminded them of. After much discussion, a consensus was reached and the teacher made additions to the drawings to make them represent the objects concerned. After this, the children were asked to tell a story that included as many of the objects as possible and initially, they worked on this together; as they were doing this many indulged in spontaneous dramatic improvisations in order to make the point. In the pieces of writing they went on to produce individually, it was evident to the teacher that their use of descriptive language devices had significantly improved.

Writing conferences

Once writing is underway, writing conferences can be used to challenge higher ability pupils. During these, they can be asked to justify the language choices they have made, or to offer critiques of other children's writing (see 'response partners' below) such as in guided writing in the Literacy Hour. Sometimes these conferences will be with the teacher or a small group of other children but, on occasions, they can take place during the plenary session of a Literacy Hour.[7]

Being a response partner

Gifted and talented children can work as response partners for the writing of children of similar or lower ability to themselves while they work in pairs, although care needs to be taken to ensure that they are not always in a lead position as this could have a negative affect on interpersonal relationships within a class. Some planning needs to go into this. Here is how to be a good 'response partner';

1. Listen carefully to your partner read his/her work.
2. Tell your partner what you liked about the writing.
3. Think how it might be improved:
   (a) Will the audience understand it?
   (b) Will they find it interesting?
   (c) Is there anything missing?
   (d) Can you suggest any words or changes?
   (e) Is it the right length?
4. Suggest how the writing might be improved.

(Fisher and Williams 2000)

Joe

Once there was a Happy Bright green frog called Ruby ribbit. Ruby was very lonely because all the animals were scared of her. It was her birthday and Ruby had put balloons all around the pond. A duck was dosing in the sun strumming his guitar when the duck was floating down the pond he poped the Balloon (BANG)! Ruby Sprang out of her reeds and landed on top of the duck with a SPLASH "Sorry" croaked Ruby. Suddenly a curious and wise snake poped out of its log home on the river bank wondering what the conversation was about.

" what are you doing can we be friends-s-s-s? he hissed. " yes please!" Spluttered Ruby. So the snake, the duck and the frog became friends the snake gave ruby a pressent it was a Sock She always wanted her sock I found it from that day on, Ruby kept her frog Spawn warm in the cosy sock and no-one ever ran away from Ruby again.

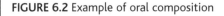

FIGURE 6.2 Example of oral composition

Collaborating with less able children can be quite a challenge for gifted and talented children as they are often highly individualistic and can become irritated if others do not keep up with their speed of thought. They need to be aware that it is important to show sensitivity towards others. This is made easier if they have been taught how roles operate within a group (see 'working in a group' above).

Some final thoughts

Speaking and listening are both vital ingredients of effective learning. They underpin learning across the curriculum. Gifted and talented children often possess sophisticated oral ability but are not always so good at listening to the views of others. If they are not challenged appropriately – in terms of either speaking or listening – they easily become disillusioned and demotivated, so it is vital that teachers respond to their needs appropriately to ensure that they remain interested in learning and fulfil their potential. Ways of achieving this have been suggested in this chapter that are not too difficult to implement in classrooms where the demands on busy teachers, who have to cater for pupils across the ability spectrum, are heavy. All children, but particularly those who are gifted and talented, need to be encouraged to think deeply about how, as well as what, they are learning as part of creative, problem-solving tasks. Specific techniques to help them achieve this have been discussed with this in mind as, without nurturing the gifts and talents of all children, society will be impoverished. In the past many geniuses came to the surface *despite* their education. Many more are likely to shine forth if appropriate attention is given to them when lessons are planned, to ensure that the talents they have are not hidden from view. Competence and confidence in 'speaking and listening' is one of the keys to unlocking this.

Acknowledgements

My thanks go to all the teachers and local authority advisers involved in the Nurturing Young Talent project for allowing me to share aspects of their work in this chapter and in particular, those who have been working in the projects in Dorset and the London Boroughs of Richmond and Hounslow.

Notes

1. The NYT project for pupils in Key Stage 1 is funded by the Gifted and Talented unit at the DfES with research support being offered by Brunel University's BACE centre. Fourteen local authorities are taking part and examples of best practice will be published in 2006.

2. See Williams (2000), for more on this.
3. See Fisher and Williams (2004) for more details.
4. This source is not actually from the Key Stage 1 NYT research project although the Medway division of Kent Local Authority is involved.
5. See DfES (2003) for suggestions for more listening activities.
6. In the early stages of the National Curriculum speaking and listening fought hard to be recognised as being of equal importance to reading and writing (see Cox 1995). It was not until 2001 that it was properly acknowledged.
7. See Williams (2002) for more about teaching in the Literacy Hour.

References and further reading

Baczala, K. (2003) *Guidance on Gifted and Talented Children in the Foundation Stage*. London: Medway Council.

Bloom, B.S. (1956) *Taxonomy of Educational Objectives*, vol. 1. London: Longman.

Browne, A. (2003) *The Shape Game*. London: Random House.

Center for Talented Youth (CTY) (1994) *Philosophy and Program Policy*. Baltimore, MD: The Johns Hopkins University.

Cox, B. (1995) *Cox on the Battle for the English Curriculum*. London: Hodder & Stoughton.

DfEE (1998) *The National Literacy Strategy: Framework for Teaching*. London: HMSO.

DfEE (1999) *The National Curriculum for England: English*. London: HMSO.

DfEE (2000a) *Curriculum Guidance for the Foundation Stage*. London: QCA.

DfEE (2000b) *National Literacy and Numeracy Strategies: Guidance on Teaching Able Children*. London: HMSO.

DfES (2003) *Speaking, Listening, Learning: Working with Children in Key Stages 1 and 2*. London: QCA.

Fisher, R. (1999) *First Stories for Thinking*. Oxford: Nash Pollock.

Fisher, R. (2001) 'Philosophy in primary schools', *Reading*, 35(2): 67–73.

Fisher, R. and Williams, M. (eds) (2004) *Unlocking Creativity: Teaching Across the Curriculum*. London: David Fulton Publishers.

Fisher, R. and Williams, M. (eds) (2006) *Unlocking Literacy* (2nd edn). London: David Fulton Publishers.

Gardner, H. (1993) *Multiple Intelligences*. New York: Basic Books.

Hodson, P. and Jones, D. (2001) *Teaching Children to Write: A Process Approach to Writing for Literacy*. London: David Fulton Publishers.

Johnson, C. (2000) 'What did I say? Speaking, listening and drama', in R. Fisher and M. Williams (eds) *Unlocking Literacy*. London: David Fulton Publishers.

Koshy, V. (2001) *Teaching Gifted Children 4–7*. London: David Fulton Publishers.

Koshy, V. and Casey, R. (1997) *Effective Provision for Able and Exceptionally Able Children*. London: Hodder & Stoughton.

Meadows, C. and Cashdan, A. (1998) *Helping Children Learning*. London: David Fulton Publishers.

Moyles, J. (2002) 'Foreword', in A. Craft (ed.) *Creativity and Early Years Education*. London: Continuum.

Ofsted (2002) *National Literacy Strategy: The First Four Years 1998–2002*. HMI 555. London: Ofsted.

QCA (2001) *Working with Gifted and Talented Children*. London: QCA.

Renzulli, J. (1994) *Schools for Talent Development*. Mansfield Centre, CT: Creative Learning Press.

Vygotsky, L.S. (1962) *Thought and Language*. Cambridge, MA: MIT Press.

Wallace, B. (2002) *Teaching Thinking Skills Across the Early Years*. London: David Fulton Publishers.

Williams, M. (2000) 'The part which metacognition can play in raising standards in English at Key Stage 2', *Reading*, 34(1): 3–8.

Williams, M. (ed.) (2002) *Unlocking Writing*. London: David Fulton Publishers.

CHAPTER 7

Dynamic talk: speaking, listening and learning through drama

Colleen Johnson

Sometimes when I'm in role, I think, 'This is how I'll talk when I'm grown up.'

(Ella, age 9)

Drama talk can be the most dynamic talk in the classroom. Through drama we can create a myriad of contexts in which children are able to experience diversity in spoken language. Such experiences can help develop skills in speaking and active listening, through paired, group and whole-class work, building children's confidence in their own oracy. The range is comprehensive and encompasses speaking as a character, planning *for* a scene, dialogue *in* performance or *responding to* performance, and whole-class discussions both *in* role and *out of* role. Such activities create excellent opportunities for assessing children's speaking and listening, using, for example, the assessment observation sheet 2 which is suggested in Chapter 8. With its potential for affording talk, which is rich with possibilities for learning, drama is a must in the classroom.

The Primary Strategies for Speaking, Listening and Literacy advocate whole-class, group and individual teaching, which engage pupils in active learning.[1] Drama can stimulate the best in whole-class teaching through discursive and interactive talk, fostered and modelled by the teacher. Through drama, the teacher can create contexts for exploratory talk, developing hypothesis and opinion.[2] Good quality independent group work can be maintained when such talk continues while the children are working without teacher support.

Drama practitioners welcome the subject's return to the curriculum and its heightened status. However, those teachers entering the profession within the past decade may well not have experienced drama in their professional training, which has largely focused on the core curriculum subjects to the detriment of Foundation subjects and the arts in particular. It is understandable then that many are reluctant to attempt to teach a subject in which they may have had insufficient grounding. For the teacher with little or no experience of drama, therefore, what follows are tried and tested approaches for the non-specialist which can be incorporated within lessons such as literacy and personal, social and moral education (PSME). All activities took place *in* the classroom. After all, in most schools, space is at a premium and access to larger areas such as the hall or the gym may be limited. In addition, such activities may easily stimulate further reading or written work. In this case it is useful for the children to be working where relevant resources are at hand.

Anita's story

A Year 4 teacher incorporated drama in her teaching of speaking and listening, literacy and moral education. She devised a scheme of activities to help children explore issues surrounding bullying. She began by showing the children a letter purported to have been written by a 13-year-old girl to her mother, before leaving home. She read:

> Dear Mum,
> It's happened again and today was worse than ever.
> Even my so-called friends are being horrible. I've had enough and I'm never going back to that school.
> Don't worry about me. I'll be OK.
> Love Anita.

Group discussion and interaction

The children were invited to suggest what might have happened to make Anita want to run away. Most were of the opinion that she must have been bullied and evidently over a period of time. There was speculation on the nature of the bullying which Anita had been experiencing. Various examples were offered including teasing, sending spiteful text messages, name calling and stealing her equipment. The children were asked to make notes on what was being discussed as these could be used later to help them in preparation for short improvised scenes.[3]

Group improvisation

The teacher organised the children into groups of five. Each group was asked to create a short dramatic representation of one of the bullying incidents which Anita may have experienced. She stressed that it was not necessary for all in the group to take part in the improvisation itself but that all should be involved in the devising process. This allows the shy or reluctant child to contribute at a level at which s/he feels comfortable.

She added that some groups may decide to show a scene which might not necessarily include the incident as it happened but could, for example, show a prank being planned, a group of teachers confronting the bullies or a conversation between Anita and those not directly involved, after the event. This added a challenging dimension to the children's discussion and led them to think beyond action-based drama to that which might involve more reflective dialogue.

The teacher directed the children to think carefully about the effect which they would like their scene to have on the audience and how they might best achieve this. For example, how could they best convey the feelings of certain characters by facial expression or by physical proximity to one another in the scene? How might they achieve suspense within the scene or deepen empathy for a particular character? Again, an added dimension was evident. Having to place themselves in the position of audience as well as directors and actors engaged the children in metacognitive process and enriched their exploratory talk.[4]

Each scene was watched in turn. The teacher encouraged the children to critically reflect upon the performances by asking them to say 'what worked well and why'. This helped the children to consider the ways in which those who had created the scene had used drama conventions such as mime, improvisation, characterisation and staging and to what effect. This reflective process fosters the growth of critical vocabulary for dramatic activity and enhances learning *in* drama.

In one scene 'Anita' had remained at a distance from the four playing her 'friends'. One child commented that this had made her 'really separate from everybody else. She is on her own.' This provoked responses from others in relation to feelings of isolation, which may be experienced by victims of bullying. In another scene, however, 'Anita' was in the middle of a tight group of 'peers' and their physical proximity heightened the claustrophobic atmosphere of the scene. A child commented, 'When they are that close, it is scary. No-one else can hear what they are saying to you.' Others said, 'You can be on your own in a group when they are all against you' and, 'They made it look like Anita was trapped.'

Encouraging the children to comment constructively on performance, the teacher led discussion about the effects within the scenes and how they had been achieved.[5] The participants were visibly gratified to hear, via the audience's feedback, how well they had succeeded. Critical appreciation and praise from peers can sometimes be more rewarding than that from teachers or other adults.

The teacher facilitated the children's learning *through* drama by asking them to make connections between what they had seen, or discussed, so far and events in their own lives. In one scene, a parent had been seen talking with her friend about how her daughter's attitude to school seemed to have changed in recent days. When discussing this scene, one child said, 'It makes you realise that if you are not happy it affects your Mum or your Dad.' And another added, 'Yes, you think you won't tell them if something's wrong but then they know something's wrong anyway and it makes it worse because they don't know what to do.' Several spoke about the sorts of bullying which they had experienced, or witnessed. The teacher encouraged them to consider examples from literature and television dramas. Here the teacher was capitalising on the children's engagement with the medium of television, which provokes animated conversation between children on a daily basis.

Written tasks followed which the children approached enthusiastically. They were required to chart the build-up of a scene in which they had taken part, or helped devise, and to write character sketches, focusing on small details to evoke sympathy or dislike.[6] Research shows drama enhances the quality of children's written work, stimulating their imagination and giving real purpose to the task in hand.[7]

Still image

The children were asked to return to their groups to make a 'still image' to represent their scene. This requires children to organise themselves into creating a three-dimensional image to represent a dramatic moment or a visual 'summing up' of a situation. This strategy serves a number of purposes:

- It helps create a visual 'aide-mémoire'.
- It is less time-consuming to view a series of still images than improvised scenes.
- It involves highly focused discussion as children negotiate both meaning and conveyance of shared meaning to an audience.
- It requires less physical movement than a whole improvised scene in preparation and is therefore a useful strategy for the teacher anxious about possible rising noise levels.

The still images were presented in an agreed chronological order and the teacher exploited further opportunities for speaking and listening by introducing another strategy.

Thought tracking

Here those in the image are invited to contribute the immediate thoughts of the characters they are representing. The teacher said, 'At this moment I am thinking...' She moved around the image touching each character on the shoulder, inviting them to speak. One image showed a group of Anita's peers talking about having hidden her lunch box. Guided by the teacher, they spoke their thoughts in turn:

> 'Brilliant – no way she will find it.'
> 'I'm glad it isn't me they are being mean to.'
> 'She'll be hungry.'
> 'Hope we don't get found out.'

Another way of combining these strategies is to have those observing volunteer the thoughts of the characters in the image. This makes an already active learning situation even more interactive. To exploit literacy links, the children could be invited to invent captions to accompany the images, to write dialogue or create diary entries for characters.

Teacher and children in role

The teacher explained that she and the children would be acting together in their drama. She would be in role as the school's head teacher. Concerned about the negative publicity which Anita's disappearance had caused for the school, the head teacher had decided to call a meeting of student counsellors, teachers and parent governors to discuss ways forward. She organised the class into three groups: parents, teachers and student counsellors and the meeting began. In role, she said,

> Welcome, everyone, to this emergency meeting. I'm delighted to say that Anita has returned home safely but her mother is insistent that she will not be returning to our school. We must recognise that we have a bullying problem here and we urgently need to do something about it.
>
> You have been invited to attend because it is recognised that all of you have some expertise to offer in helping develop a policy on bullying. I suggest that we begin by dividing into our groups. Would each allocate a leader to head up the discussion and a scribe to make notes and to write up agreed key points, in order to feed back to us all when we reconvene?

She was using formal language to set the tone and to underline the seriousness of the endeavour. The status of the role of 'the head' helps the teacher feel in control of the class while working within the drama. Similar status roles in other dramas might include detective inspector, business manager or expedition leader.

The mantle of the expert

Here the children took on the role of 'experts' with knowledge and experience collectively greater than those of the teacher in role. When children adopt the mantle of the expert, the roles of teacher and pupil are temporarily reversed. The children are the 'ones in the know', who have the expertise to apply to the task in hand – in this case, helping develop a working anti-bullying policy – while the teacher in a higher status role, nevertheless, is the 'one who needs to know' seeking their help and guidance.[8]

Children in role as experts rise to the challenge of using spoken language appropriate to a situation, which is uniquely afforded them through drama. They are *in* the role of another – usually an adult or older child – but it is still their own use of language demanded by that role which is being nurtured. It is important for the teacher to encourage reflection, out of role, on the levels of sophistication and quality of the language some children are able to demonstrate in role, especially as experts, and for the children to consider how they access such language, a metacognitive process fundamental to learning. As one child said, 'Sometimes when I'm in role I think, "This is how I'll talk when I'm grown up."'

Back in the whole group, individuals fed back on behalf of their cohort. The 'student counsellors' made several suggestions, including the implementation of 'buddy systems' where younger and less confident children might be befriended by older students, who would 'look out' for them and offer support and guidance.

The 'teachers' suggested that more could be done in the classroom to raise awareness about the effects of bullying on victims. One 'teacher' said, 'We should have films about what happens when they run away from home.' Another said, 'Some children just think they are having a joke. They don't mean to really hurt.' Another added, 'I agree. Sometimes they think they are only teasing but they don't mean to be really nasty.'

The 'parents' offered their perspective, 'We want more meetings with the teachers because sometimes your children don't tell you anything about what's going on at school.' And, 'If we don't sort it out, people won't send their children to this school.' This was serious, purposeful talk. Ground rules for dialogue were observed, children responded appropriately to the contributions of others in the light of alternative viewpoints and spoken argument was clearly presented.[9] Opinions were qualified and agreements were reached. The activity demonstrated the quality of learning achievable through exploratory talk facilitated by, in this case, the strategies of teacher in role and mantle of the expert.

Out of role, the children were encouraged to reflect upon the range of talk in which they had been engaged and to consider how their own use of language appropriate to the role had given the drama credibility. Discussion showed raised awareness of the effects of bullying upon the immediate victim, families and the community. The children, through their roles, had been able to identify proactive strategies for creating a school ethos which would make bullying less likely to thrive. The role of the 'innocent bystander' was explored and the ways in which s/he becomes part of the problem if s/he doesn't go to the aid of the victim or, more realistically, to get help from someone else, usually an adult. The activity demonstrates how powerful a tool drama can be in facilitating personal, social and moral development.

The Gruffalo's Child

A Year 1/2 (vertically grouped) class had been reading *The Gruffalo's Child* by Julie Donaldson and Axel Scheffler.[10] This is the story of a bored young creature, the Gruffalo's child, whose curiosity gets the better of her. Despite warnings from her father, the Gruffalo, she heads off into the deep dark wood in search of the Big Bad Mouse, where she experiences the fright of her life.

The teacher used a number of drama strategies in order to develop the children's ability to listen with concentration, to use talk in order to plan effectively, to work collaboratively and to act out well-known stories.[11] She began by recapping on the first part of the story when the Gruffalo was warning his daughter about the wood and showing the illustration of that moment. She asked the children to listen carefully to the description of the Big Bad Mouse because 'they [the children] would all be playing the part soon'. She read:

> 'The Gruffalo said that no gruffalo should
> Ever set foot in the deep dark wood.
> 'Why not? Why not?' *'Because if you do*
> *The Big Bad Mouse will be after you.*
> *I met him once,'* said the Gruffalo.
> *'I met him a long time ago.'*
> 'What does he look like? Tell us, Dad.
> 'Is he terribly big and terribly bad?'
> *'I can't quite remember,'* the Gruffalo said.
> *'The Big Bad Mouse is terribly strong*
> *And his scaly tail is terribly long.*
> *His eyes are like pools of terrible fire*
> *And his terrible whiskers are tougher than wire.'*

She asked the children to find a space in order to pretend that they were each the Big Bad Mouse. She said, 'On the first signal [the shaking of a tambourine] you can move around – and remember, the Big Bad Mouse moves quietly through the woods – but on the second signal you must freeze.' The children spent some time moving around and getting into character. The description of the Big Bad Mouse makes him 'larger than life' and is therefore ideal for such an activity with Key Stage 1 children who enjoy creating exaggerated movements in order to represent giants and monsters.

She said, 'If the Big Bad Mouse could speak, what would he say?' As she moved between the children she invited some of them in turn to speak:

> 'I'll eat you up.'
> 'Keep away from my woods.'
> 'I like to scare gruffalos.'
> 'Grrrowl!'

Then she made an opportunity for the children to see each other's work so far. She asked those in one half of the room to 'freeze' so that those in the other half could look at the various Big Bad Mice. She asked them to comment on what they were seeing with, 'What words come into your head when you look at the Big Bad Mouse?' and, 'How would you describe the look on this Mouse's face?' There were several comments:

'I like Nerssi's because how he stares make his eyes pools of fire.'
'Anna's making her hands like claws – her fingers are jagged.'
'That one [pointing to a Mouse crouching behind a table] is very
frightening because he is ready to pounce.'

The children were learning to comment critically on performance and those 'freezing' in character were learning about how what they were doing was impacting upon their audience.

Teacher and children in role

The teacher explained that she would now be playing the part of the Gruffalo and that they would be the Gruffalo's children. They were to try to persuade her to let them go into the wood. She suggested that they turn to each other to discuss possible persuasive arguments. After a few minutes, the whole-class improvisation began.

> 'Please, Dad, can I go to the wood?'
> 'It's too dark in there.'
> 'Can I go with a torch?'
> 'Absolutely not.'
> 'Can I go with my friend?'
> 'No, no.'
> 'I will take some cheese for the mouse'.
> 'No. He will still be after you.'

It was evident that permission would not be granted so, out of role, the teacher suggested that, just as in the book, they consider going without their Dad's permission. She introduced the next strategy.

Conscience alley

This strategy allows children to explore the moral dilemma within a story or a situation and to articulate and explore conflicting viewpoints. In this case, they were to consider the reasons both for and against setting off into the woods. The teacher organised the children into two lines facing each other. She said, 'You are all Gruffalo children. Those of you in this line [pointing to the one on the left] are going to give reasons *for* going into the deep dark wood and those of you in this line [the one on the right] are going to give reasons for *not* going.' She gave them some time to think and then she moved down the line inviting each child to speak, one at a time, first from the left line, second from the right, and so on. Their responses began as follows:

> 'I want to meet the Big Bad Mouse.'
> 'Dad says don't go.'
> 'We can go together.'
> 'Then I'll be in trouble.'
> 'We can go at night when he's asleep.'
> 'I'm scared.'
> 'We can take a torch.'
> 'Then the Big Bad Mouse will see us.'

This process helps generate new thinking and a range of views but for the less confident child who is challenged by having to think on the spot in this way, s/he can simply repeat a statement already made, therefore requiring concentrated listening.

At the end of the conscience alley exercise, the teacher gave the children opportunities to discuss some of the reasons offered both for and against the journey and asked if the activity had made them think of anything in their own lives, or in books and on television. One child talked about the film of J. K. Rowling's first Harry Potter Book, *Harry Potter and the Philosopher's Stone*.[12] He said, 'Harry went back to find Hermione but everybody had to leave the school, but he did it.' Several children had seen the film and were keen to discuss that incident. The teacher asked them what they thought about Harry's decision to disobey on that occasion. There was animated discussion and several points of view were given:

> 'Well, he shouldn't have done it because it was dangerous.'
> 'She was his friend so that's fair.'
> 'He does magic, so he is OK.'

'He did it for the right reasons.'
'But what if he'd been killed?'
'Then there wouldn't be any more Harry Potter books!'

This last comment provoked gasps of horror, as well as laughter!

These young children were engaging in debate on moral issues. The teacher ended the activity by saying that it was clear that there was determination from several Gruffalo children to go on the adventure so, in their next drama, they would all be playing those who had decided to go.

Whole-class improvisation

The teacher gathered the children on the carpet and explained that in their drama she would now be acting alongside them as a Gruffalo child. She reminded them that as their Gruffalo Dad wouldn't allow them into the wood they would have to go without him finding out. She asked, 'How should we do this?' and the children offered suggestions about creeping quietly out of the house so as not to disturb the Gruffalo. Stories in which people are required to move quietly with stealth are useful in the Key Stage 1 classroom for both helping the teacher feel 'in control' and keeping the noise level down so as not to disturb other classes. This is where a classroom full of furniture becomes a valuable resource for the story: it serves both as an interior of a house through which the children must move quietly and as the dark wood with bushes and trees to provide hiding places and cover.

The teacher began by reading from the story:

> One snowy night when the Gruffalo snored
> The Gruffalo's Child was feeling bored.
> The Gruffalo's Child was feeling brave
> So she tiptoed out of the gruffalo cave.
> The snow fell fast and the wind blew wild.
> Into the wood went the Gruffalo's Child.

As the children moved through the 'wood' she asked them to 'freeze'. She introduced the thought tracking strategy, saying, 'As I entered the deep dark wood, I thought to myself...' She invited each child to speak the character's thoughts aloud as she moved among them. They responded:

> I feel shaky.
> I don't want to see a ghost.
> What will happen to me?
> I hope I meet the Mouse!
> My dad will be very angry.

Upon their safe return from the encounter with the 'Big Bad Mouse' the teacher invited the children to go beyond the usual end of the story. One of Scheffler's illustrations shows how the little mouse had been able to dupe the Gruffalo's child into thinking he really was a Big Bad Mouse. He had climbed a tree and positioned himself so that the light from the moon fell upon him and cast a long shadow on the ground, making himself appear enormous.

Paired work

The teacher organised the children into pairs: one child was to play the Gruffalo Dad and the other, the Gruffalo's child. She set the scene:

'The Gruffalo Dad has woken to find his child missing. He is worried and cross, hoping and waiting for her return.'

Her instructions to the Gruffalo's children were:

'If you find your Dad awake, although he will be angry, at least you can explain to him how the little mouse had tricked him to thinking he was a Big Bad Mouse, then perhaps he will no longer be afraid to go into the deep dark wood.'

This activity demanded sophisticated use of subject-specific language and could be used to help the teacher assess levels of understanding in relation to how shadows are created and vary in size.[13] This is an example of how drama can inform assessment in other curriculum areas, such as science. By going on an imaginative journey beyond the traditional end of the story, the children were able to enlighten the Gruffalo with their expert knowledge and understanding.

Each of the drama activities explored in the two examples above can be delivered within a lesson, and need not necessarily occur on the same day. In fact, giving time for children to think back on what they have done in their previous drama can lead to further reflective talk, and allows for what Fisher calls 'soft thinking',[14] that which takes place over days rather than hours. The strategies can be applied to the exploration of other themes and texts and throughout the primary school. The processes of drama are largely transferable between different ages and Key Stages. The levels of sophistication of the language used will be dictated by the maturity of the group and by the teacher's skill in guiding and challenging the children's thinking.[15]

With imagination and willingness to take the occasional risk, the primary teacher will benefit enormously from adding drama to her teaching repertoire. If teachers are to create 'sparks that make learning vivid'[16] in the classroom, then drama is the box of matches.

The best bit of drama was I talked like the Gruffalo and it was weird and wonderful.

(Thomas, age 6)

Notes

1. DfEE (1998, 2004).
2. Johnson (2000).
3. NLS Y4 Writing objectives: relating to note taking.
4. Johnson (2004).
5. S, L & L Y4 t1 Drama objective: Children are required to comment constructively on plays & performance.
6. NLS Y4 t1 text level work.
7. Johnson (2002).
8. Johnson (2000) explores Dorothy Heathcote's 'mantle of the expert' approach in the classroom.
9. S, L & L Y4 objectives including speaking and listening.
10. Donaldson and Scheffler (2004).
11. S, L & L Ys 1 and 2 objectives, covering speaking, listening, group discussion and interaction and drama.
12. Rowling (2004).
13. See National Curriculum for units 1D: Light and Dark to 3F: Light and Shadows, London: QCA.
14. Fisher (2004).
15. Johnson (2004).
16. DfES (2003).

References and further reading

Clipson-Boyles, S. (1998) *Drama in Primary English Teaching*. London: David Fulton Publishers.

DfEE (1998) *The National Literacy Strategy: Framework for Teaching*. London: HMSO.

DfEE (2004) *The Primary National Strategy: Speaking, Listening, Learning*. London: QCA.

DfES (1999) *Opportunities for Drama in the Framework of Objectives*. London: HMSO.

DfES (2003) *Excellence and Enjoyment: A Strategy for Primary Schools*. London: HMSO.

Donaldson, J. and Scheffler, A. (2004) *The Gruffalo's Child*. London: Macmillan.

Fisher, R. (2004) 'What is creativity?', in R. Fisher and M. Williams (eds) *Unlocking Creativity: Teaching Across the Curriculum*. London: David Fulton Publishers.

Fleming, M. (1994) *Starting Drama Teaching*. London: David Fulton Publishers.

Heathcote, D. and Bolton, G. (1995) *Drama for Learning: An Account of Dorothy Heathcote's 'Mantle of the Expert' Approach to Education*. Portsmouth, NH: Heinemann.

Hendy, L. and Toon, L. (2001) *Supporting Drama and Imaginative Play in the Early Years*. Buckingham: Open University Press.

Johnson, C. (2000) 'What did I say? Speaking, listening and drama', in R. Fisher and M. Williams (eds) *Unlocking Literacy*. London: David Fulton Publishers.

Johnson, C. (2002) 'Writing aloud: drama and writing', in M. Williams (ed.) *Unlocking Writing*. London: David Fulton Publishers.

Johnson, C. (2004) 'Creative drama: thinking from within', in R. Fisher and M. Williams (eds) *Unlocking Creativity: Teaching Across the Curriculum*. London: David Fulton Publishers.

Rowling, J.K. (2004) *Harry Potter and the Philosopher's Stone*. London: Bloomsbury.

Winston, J. (2000) *Drama, Literacy and Moral Education 5–11*. London: David Fulton Publishers.

Winston, J. and Tandy, M. (2001) *Beginning Drama 4–11*. London: David Fulton Publishers.

Woolland, B. (2003) *The Teaching of Drama in the Primary School*. Harlow: Longman.

Speaking and listening: planning and assessment

Deborah Jones

When I talk my thoughts click.

(Jess, age 8)

Introduction

There is a sense in which all of us are helped by articulating our thoughts. It is often within the process of explaining or describing what we think, that our thoughts 'click' into place and we understand what we already know. In other words, making our implicit thoughts explicit through talk is a powerful learning tool for both adults and children. It may be assumed that because talk is interwoven into the fabric of the classroom and daily life in general, that competence develops 'naturally' and without the need for explicit teaching. By contrast, this chapter will highlight the importance of rigorous planning for speaking and listening and in addition the need to plan in specific and regular opportunities for assessing this area.

At the most basic level, then, one of the ways teachers can assess what children know and understand is by listening to children talking, that is, assessment through talk. At another level, however, as teachers we are engaged in developing children's talk and therefore need to assess their competence in this regard. In this sense we are to assess the talk itself. So, the process of planning for and assessing speaking and listening, as part of the curriculum, is one which is multi-faceted. Effective planning and assessment can be a rich experience in terms of what it yields for both children and teachers.

Current context

National Curriculum assessment has undergone many changes since its introduction. Each year, handbooks of guidance (DfES 2005) are published, laying down the statutory assessment requirements for each Key Stage.[1] Both summative assessment (measuring attainment after teaching and learning) and formative assessment (informing the teaching and learning processes) are required.

There have been several important influences on the way assessment is approached. As a result of extensive research, Black and Wiliam[2] found that formative assessment strategies raise standards of attainment and produced five key factors that improve learning through assessment:

- the provision of effective feedback to pupils;
- the active involvement of pupils in their own learning;
- adjusting teaching according to assessment results;
- recognising the huge influence assessment has on pupils' self-esteem and motivation;
- the need for pupils to be able to assess themselves and understand how to improve.

Other important factors for formative assessment were also noted:

- sharing learning goals with pupils;
- involving pupils in self-assessment;
- providing feedback which enables pupils to recognise and take the next steps.

Based on this research, Clarke[3] has drawn out additional aspects of formative assessment as follows:

- focusing feedback around learning intentions;
- organising appropriate target setting;
- raising children's self-esteem throughout.

In 2002, the Assessment Reform Group produced 'Assessment for Learning: 10 Principles'.[4] In addition, QCA 'Assessment for Learning' materials have been provided for teacher support. An important distinction has been made, 'Assessment for Learning' being defined as the process of classroom assessment to improve learning, whereas assessment of learning is defined as the measurement of what children can do.[5]

All these initiatives have impacted greatly not only on how assessment is perceived, but also upon how assessment in schools is carried out.

Approaches to planning and assessing speaking and listening

Currently, within the English National Curriculum, children are required to undergo both standardised assessments and teacher assessments for Reading and

Writing, but teacher assessment only for Speaking and Listening. Criteria for assessment may be found as level descriptions within the *English in the National Curriculum* (DfEE 2000). More recently, documentation, *Speaking, Listening, Learning: Working with Children in Key Stages 1 and 2* (DfES 2003)[6] has been produced by the Primary National Strategy. It relates Speaking and Listening to the programmes of study in the English National Curriculum and presents four strands: Speaking, Listening, Group discussion and interaction, and Drama. Teaching objectives are provided that cover these four strands across the various terms and years. This package offers brief guidelines for the assessment of the four strands and includes a generic record sheet for teacher use. Whereas some useful suggestions are made here, it states teachers, when assessing children, should be clear that 'it is not their accent or dialect that is being assessed, the length of their contribution, the opinion expressed or their confidence' (DfES 2003: 30). Herein lies the difficulty in reducing the richness and complexity of Speaking and Listening to a set of objectives. Aspects such as confidence, self-esteem, gender, dialects and languages spoken are all crucial to any assessments we make in this area (further consideration will be given to this below).

At the heart of any effective approach to the assessment of speaking and listening are two main aspects. First, a set of clear criteria on which to base observations and, second, the way in which these assessments enable the teacher to plan the next learning steps. One example of a particularly useful method which incorporates these aspects is to be found in the First Steps materials.[7] These include a Developmental Continuum of aspects of speaking and listening, which can be used to record children's development and see progression clearly. In addition, helpful teaching emphases are included which parallel the various stages of development and aim to move children on. This provides not only a clear framework but also a rigorous approach to formative assessment.

The principles of assessment

There are certain principles which must inform our assessment practice, whatever the curricular area. These will necessarily reflect our approach to teaching and learning, as assessment is inextricably linked to both of these.

First, assessment should be continuous. Any assessments undertaken should take place over a period of time, in part, to give children the best possible chance of showing what they can do and also to build up a picture of progression and development over time.

Second, assessment should be curricular. Assessments need to be related to what children are currently learning and take place within a strong context of meaning, unlike some forms of traditional assessment which are bolt-on activities, quite unrelated to classroom work.

Next, assessment should be consultative. Assessment is not something the adult does to the child, rather it is a supportive, collaborative process, shared between a range of people. Input from children, parents/carers, teachers and other adults is all a useful part of practice.

Finally, assessment should be communicative. Feedback by teachers to children or between peers, whether oral or written, should communicate clearly, as should assessment documentation. These should be adapted to the audience, for example, reports for parents need to be jargon-free. It is essential that shared understandings are established and maintained.

Planning for speaking and listening

Aspects of talk

When planning for talk, it is important to consider the nature of talk and in so doing to identify four discrete, but interdependent aspects of speaking and listening:

- *social*: for developing relationships;
- *communicative*: for transferring meaning;
- *cultural*: when different meanings are adopted by different speech communities; among children these might be associated with popular culture;
- *cognitive*: using talk as a means of learning.

As teachers, we can plan to develop any of these aspects, indeed, all these need to progress if a child is to become a well-rounded speaker. Children need to learn about the social elements of talk, the expression of feelings, the development of relationships and how additional aspects such as body language work with talk in order to develop such relationships and affect or sharpen our communication.

The use of drama or circle time can be crucial for extending children's understandings of these aspects (see Chapter 7) But the cognitive aspect is fundamental. In planning for effective speaking and listening opportunities, then, we are also planning for effective learning. One way in which this can be done, is by focusing on exploratory talk. As the National Oracy Project points out:[8]

> Learning is the product of the interaction between the old and the new, the known and the not known…through talk it is possible to explore and clarify new meanings, review and revise old meanings, until there can be an accommodation between the two.

(Norman 1992: 41)

Research by Mercer[9] highlights the value of this kind of exploratory talk but notes that observational research indicates very little of it occurs naturally in the classroom. However, research from Australia (Cormack *et al.* 1998)[10] shows that, despite fears from teachers that children would not be focused, when children were provided with structured opportunities to work with their peers, they were able to use speaking and listening to do the following:

- interrogate their own understanding;
- aid recall;
- instruct others;
- work on ideas and propositions;
- problematise;
- argue a personal point of view;
- rehearse subject-specific language;
- progressively shape knowledge;
- generate ideas;
- 'sponsor' learning.

The research also highlights that this effective use of speaking and listening for cognitive purposes was dependent on the clarity of the task (children knew what kind of talk was required) and an appropriate selection of topic which allowed children to build on their previous knowledge and understanding.

These aspects can form the basis of an effective teacher checklist when planning for exploratory talk in the classroom (Table 8.1).

Audience and purpose

Several schools which are implementing the new guidance have started by focusing on current practice in relation to the development of children's spoken language. In doing so, they have adopted the functional approach to language which is evident in the Professional Development materials for the guidance (DfES 2003: 39). This approach is based on functional linguistics[11] where the structure of the language we use and the structure of the social action are mutually determining. Put simply, we vary what we say and how we say it according to who we are with (the audience) and why we are speaking (the purpose). For children, development and progression in their speaking and listening skills are marked by an increasing confidence and competence in achieving these aims.

A preliminary analysis of the kinds of speaking and listening children engage in at the beginning of the school day could look like Table 8.2.

Table 8.1 Planning for exploratory talk teacher checklist

Activity:		
Learning intention:	**?**	**Comments (How?)**
Do the children know: ● *What* to do? ● *Why* they're doing it?		
Does the activity enable the children to: ● Interrogate their own understanding; ● Aid recall; ● Instruct others; ● Work on ideas and propositions; ● Problematise; ● Argue a personal point of view; ● Rehearse subject-specific language; ● Progressively shape knowledge; ● Generate ideas; ● 'Sponsor' learning.		

Again, observational evidence would seem to indicate that although children may implicitly be able to vary how they speak according to whom they are with, the opportunities for extending their speaking and listening repertoire need careful planning. Table 8.3 may provide a useful checklist/planning sheet for the types of talk experience which are offered to children. Clearly to develop this area effectively, the aspects below need to be routinely monitored.

The NOP states that 'the quality of children's talk is greatly affected by features not necessarily related to their oral ability' (1992: 76). As a result, it is not enough to note the teaching and assessment objectives alone, rather, consideration of a wider range of factors needs to take place. For example, see Table 8.4.

If we are to gain a comprehensive picture of the child's abilities in this regard, then all these aspects need to be considered and it is part of the teachers' role to act in the light of any factors which may be impeding pupils' development and performance.

Table 8.2 Children's speaking and listening at the start of the school day

Activity	Audience	Purpose	Setting
Arriving at school with parents/carers	Parents/carers	To say goodbye To reaffirm arrangements for after school Social and communicative	Playground
Meeting friends	Peers	To share information To re-establish relationships Social, communicative, cultural	Playground
Teacher greeting pupils	Teacher	To greet Communicative	Classroom
Circle Time	Teacher/teaching assistant	To listen to other children To give a sustained, individual account/anecdote/story Communicative	Classroom

Table 8.3 Planning for talk checklist: contexts planner

Activity	Audience (size/status, etc.)	Purpose	Setting

Table 8.4 Planning for talk checklist: wider factors

How will the following impact on individuals/groups? Child/group_____	
Gender	
Group size	
Personality	
Confidence	
Self-esteem	
Competence in additional languages	
Use of non-standard dialects	

To reiterate, planning, teaching, learning and assessing are parts of a cycle. All elements are interdependent, therefore it is vital that teachers have observed and assessed children's speaking and listening development in order to plan for progression. It is important that planning for teaching and planning for assessment should happen together. Fundamentally, speaking and listening should be embedded in the curriculum and not be a 'bolt-on', decontextualised activity. Teachers need to identify areas of the curriculum where the activities and the children's learning would be aided by speaking and listening. It is important to consider all curriculum areas, not just English, as talk is integral to all subjects. Assessments of talk can be planned for during collaborative science investigations, for example. In addition, teachers should identify where aspects of speaking and listening should have an explicit focus as part of the English curriculum. Some speaking and listening activities may need to be planned for over an extended period of time whereas others may constitute just a part of one lesson. All plans should do the following:

- Identify assessment objectives which are clearly linked to teaching and learning objectives/intentions (WHAT).
- Specify which children (individuals/groups) are to be assessed (WHO).
- Indicate the method of assessment and recording mechanism (HOW).
- Timing – that is, at which point assessment should take place and how long it should last (WHEN).

If assessment is to be effective, all these aspects must be considered.

Managing assessment

A key factor is that assessment opportunities must be identified and written in on all plans as part of the initial planning process. It is true to say that unless this happens, assessment will become haphazard and difficult to manage. It needs to be built into the routines and structures of the classroom. Some teachers have found it useful to annotate their weekly plans with the symbol 'A' (for assessment) to indicate exactly when it will take place.

Assessing in whole-class time

It is notoriously difficult to assess when whole-class teaching because there are so many elements for the teacher to consider. However, with careful planning, certain aspects may usefully be focused upon. The use of targeted questions, for example, can provide helpful insights into children's development in terms of their cognitive understanding and also with regard to their competence in speaking and listening. As part of the formative assessment cycle, teachers can employ different levels of questioning in order to further a child's understanding or to develop their competence. In these sessions it is usually only possible to direct questions towards and note responses of one or two children. Using an AOT (adult other than teacher) to observe and record can be invaluable.

Tables 8.5 and 8.6 can be used for focused assessments when working with small groups. It should be noted that assessment of speaking and listening can take place in any curricular area, not just in literacy sessions.

Clearly, activities designed to facilitate talk and collaboration will be best; for example, DARTS activities such as the cloze procedure sonnet (see Chapter 1) provide ample opportunity for observing and recording an individual child's speaking and listening behaviour (Figure 8.1). Observation sheet 2 in Figure 8.1 is ideal for use in this context and provides tangible snapshot evidence of the child's abilities.

Table 8.5 Targeted question sheet

Date: _____

Child: _____

Assessment objective: _____

Question (inc type)	Child response	Comment

Table 8.6 Small-group assessment

SMALL-GROUP S/L OBSERVATION SHEET 1

Date: _____

Assessment objective: _____

Name of child	Observation and development points

SMALL GROUP S/L OBSERVATION SHEET 2

TICK FEATURES OBSERVED, THEN COMPLETE
S/L DESCRIPTION AND ANALYSIS

**Look for signs of
evaluative and
reflective thinking:**

questioning
commenting
repeating
participating
describing
responding
reinforcing
suggesting
…
arguing
discussing
requesting
reasoning
persuading
conceding
encouraging
…

reflecting
…

NAME:

DATE:

ACTIVITY: SIZE OF
                                    GROUP

S/L DESCRIPTION AND ANALYSIS

AREAS FOR DEVELOPMENT

supporting
asserting
planning
collaborating
initiating
narrating
sequencing
stating
…
speculating
hypothesising
negotiating
justifying
categorising
recalling
comparing
…

Look for communication strategies:

listening attentively
body language
gestures
eye contact
facial expression

awareness of
audience
bludgeoning
causing silences
…

FIGURE 8.1 Observation of an individual child's speaking and listening behaviour

Involving children in their own learning

At the heart of these initiatives is the realisation that the most powerful learners are those who have control over their own learning.

Why self-assessment?

Central to the notion of self-assessment is the belief that we learn best through interacting with others. More specifically, Vygotsky[12] describes the 'zone of proximal development', that is, the gap between what children can do on their own and what they can do with the help of a more competent individual. So, with assistance, children can reach a higher level of attainment than they could do alone. This involves the more competent adult (possibly teacher, other adult or peer) interacting with children as a focused part of the teaching and learning process. Linked to this is the work of Sadler (1989)[13] who notes that formative assessment is dependent on two elements. First, the learner needs to understand the gap between a learning goal and his or her current level and second, there is a need for the learner to close this gap up. As Black *et al.* (2003: 14)[14] state, 'although the teacher can stimulate and guide this process, the learning has to be done by the student'. This is not just about implementing strategies; this is about defining beliefs about teaching, learning and assessing, and setting up a classroom culture where pedagogy is clearly linked to those beliefs.

In practice, this means that planning and assessment need to be shared with children so that they are 'let in' on the processes of teaching and learning. As a result, learning intentions will be communicated to children in a language they can understand. Pupils need to know not only what activities they are required to do, but also why they need to do them and what the success criteria will be. These strategies will ensure that children are not learning in a vacuum. Rather, they will be certain of what they are doing, why they are doing it, and how successful they are being in the process. By identifying and sharing these aspects, any feedback/discussion of learning between teacher and pupil will have a clear framework. It is important that teachers explain to children what assessment is and why it needs to be done, equally, that it is a shared process. Setting up the classroom environment, then, where children are free to make mistakes without recrimination and where errors will be viewed as part of the learning process, is essential. Risk-free environments are fundamental to dynamic teaching/learning/assessment contexts where children have shared control over their own learning.

In summary, then, steps to follow in order to establish a successful teaching/learning/assessing context are as follows:

1 Set up a risk-free environment where children's self-esteem is built up.

2 Explain what assessment is and why it is important.

3 Share learning intentions in a language children can understand. This should include what is to be done and why.

4 Describe the success criteria.

5 Enable children to evaluate their work in relation to the success criteria.

6 Have shared feedback between teacher and child.

7 Set targets together.

8 Reflect on the learning throughout.

Self-assessment and talk

Self-assessment and talk is a particularly sensitive area. The ways in which we talk, the languages we speak or dialects we use are part of our identity and form a large part of who we are. As such, we can become very vulnerable when our talk is opened up for scrutiny. Children, in particular, need to know that assessment of their speaking and listening skills is part of a process designed to help them. They should know that formative assessment will enable them to express themselves more effectively, develop their repertoires of talk and expand their registers of talk, in ways which enable them to exercise control over situations. It is worth explaining to children that sometimes written assessments do not demonstrate real understanding of their capabilities because these are always mediated through writing. Being part of the assessment process and learning to assess themselves can be an enormously positive experience for children, an experience which not only involves them in their own learning but also enhances their self-esteem. Making these aspects explicit to children and discussing the power of spoken language with them is a crucial part of the classroom where children are learning effectively not only about talk, but how to talk. In this area, more than any other, setting up a risk-free environment where self-esteem remains intact is of paramount importance. Children need to know that effective speakers and listeners can become powerful learners, teachers and citizens.

Peer assessment

Closely aligned to self-assessment is peer assessment where children can work through several of the stages above, together. When setting up a system for peer assessment, ground rules should be clearly decided upon and established as part of a democratic classroom process, for example, peer assessment ground rules could be:

- Respect each other.
- Respect each other's work.
- Be clear on the learning intentions.
- Read/examine the work carefully.
- Ask questions.
- Listen carefully to answers.
- Give feedback with your reasons.
- Discuss targets/ways forward together.
- Reflect.

When specifically focusing on talk, further ground rules may be as follows:

- Find out how many languages are spoken.
- Respect accents and dialects.
- Be sensitive if people lack confidence in talking.
- Give everyone a chance to talk.
- Make sure you understand what people mean.

Clearly, the above will need discussion and explanation, but all this will help establish a climate where children can come to understand that the way in which we speak actually forms part of our identity as human beings and as such are not to be ridiculed or denigrated. This, as emphasised, is a sensitive area which will need constant reinforcement.

Reflecting on talk (my own and others')

I could hardly believe how children's own talk came on in leaps and bounds as a result of watching others talk and then discussing it – it was incredible!

(Year 5 teacher)

In one classroom, the teacher was developing a programme whereby children could observe and participate in the power of spoken language. This was a project which effectively combined both peer and self-assessment and relied heavily upon discussion and reflection as a means of developing understandings. Children watched a range of video extracts in which different speakers were having a variety of effects on different audiences in different contexts and used the grids in Figure 8.2 to focus their observation and reflection. Contexts were on a continuum and ranged from the formal to the informal, for example, from the law court to the family setting. Watching others engaged in dialogue and making comments on it

WHERE? _____

WHY? (purpose for talk) _____

WHO?	HOW? (pitch, volume, tone, accent, body language)
SPEAKER 1 _____	
SPEAKER 2 _____	

EFFECTS (what and why)

SPEAKER 1 ON SPEAKER 2

SPEAKER 2 ON SPEAKER 1

YOUR FEELINGS (what and why)

IF YOU WERE SPEAKER 1

IF YOU WERE SPEAKER 2

VERDICT

HOW EFFECTIVE WAS SPEAKER 1? WHY?

HOW EFFECTIVE WAS SPEAKER 2? WHY?

FIGURE 8.2 Reflecting on talk: contexts, audiences, purposes

enabled the children to remove themselves from the situation to begin with, until they became more confident and felt able to comment on their own talk. Role play was an effective step in the process, where children were given situation cards and were asked to act them out. Usually they were given planning time when they used the grids to decide how to play their parts. These activities were set up with an observer, who then discussed the situation with the participants after, or even at, various freeze-frame stages throughout. In this particular classroom the teacher initially modelled the role of the observer/questioner with the whole class in order to help children understand the nature of the activity. Different aspects were focused upon during the course of the project, for example, accent, body language, etc. and more were added in as the project developed.

As part of their ongoing work in the classroom, children regularly reflected on and monitored their roles as speakers and listeners when working as part of a group. Table 8.7 is an example of one very simple sheet they used to focus their reflections.

Written and oral reflections on talk, their own and other people's, is a vital way of moving children on in their learning. It is often within reflection that children make explicit, for the first time, their developing understandings about the nature of talk, and about their abilities to use it effectively.

Table 8.7 Reflection: working in a group

	Yes	No	Comments/Reasons
I listened to others			
I asked other people's opinions			
I waited for a turn to speak			
I managed to make my points			
I was the leader			
I was a supporter			
I helped others by explaining			
NEXT TIME....... (How could I improve?)			

Some final reflections

Ofsted's recent review of inspection evidence claims that the weakest element of teaching is consistently the use of assessment. As a result, few pupils have an understanding of what it actually means to be good at speaking and listening.[15] However, current documentation suggests that the integration of speaking and listening into planning for literacy should be both systematic and automatic.[16] In this regard there is much work to be done.

Speaking and listening are fundamental to learning and teaching. Talk is both a means of learning and an aspect to be developed and refined in its own right. It is also a powerful tool for communicating thoughts, expressing feelings, exercising power and generally developing our identities as human beings. Within the classroom, both assessment of and through talk is vital. One teacher describes her own assessment learning curve:

> When I first assessed my children using oracy as the medium, not writing, not only did I realise how much I underestimated their knowledge and understanding, but they even looked different. Assessing through talk makes you focus on the child.
>
> (Year 2 teacher)

Assessing talk provides immediacy of access into the child's mind and a unique window into the learning process. For this reason alone, it deserves both our consideration and commitment.

Notes

1. Handbooks of guidance for assessment are produced each year for each Key Stage, e.g. DfEE (2005) *Assessment and Reporting Arrangements.*
2. Research on assessment and learning by Paul Black and Dylan Wiliam is recorded in the following document: Assessment Reform Group (1999) *Assessment for Learning: Beyond the Black Box.*
3. Clarke (2004) underscores the importance of sharing specific learning intentions with children in a language which is accessible to them.
4. The document 'Assessment for Learning: 10 Principles' is available for download at http://www.assessment-reform-group.or.uk/publications.html
5. 'Assessment for Learning' materials produced by the QCA may be accessed from http://www.qca.org.uk/10009.html
6. Brief reference to assessment is made in DfES (2003).
7. Developmental continua for reading, writing and oracy are included in the *First Steps* materials (Raison 1996) and published by Longman.
8. NOP (Norman 1992) provides a clear rationale for talk in the classroom context, together with useful strategies for developing this area.
9. Mercer (2000).
10. This research is part of the *Classroom Discourse Project,* undertaken in Australia in 1998. It can be accessed from www.griffith.edu.au/schools/cls/clearinghouse/1998classroom/cal.pdf
11. Halliday (1978).

12. More on the zone of proximal development can be found in Vygotsky (1978).
13. The theoretical position of Sadler has greatly informed understandings about assessment in education. An influencial text is Sadler (1998).
14. The book by Black *et al.* (2003) provides a useful expansion of previous booklets.
15. Useful findings on the teaching of English can be found in 'English 2000–05: a review of inspection evidence'. HMI.
16. The importance of planning and assessing speaking and listening is highlighted in the following document: 'The United Kingdom Literacy Association Response to QCA's English 21 Initiative'. This is available from http://www.ukla.org/site/publications/papers/7.php

References and further reading

'Assessment for Learning: 10 Principles', available at: http://www.assessment-reform-group.org.uk/publications.html

Assessment Reform Group (1999) *Assessment for Learning: Beyond the Black Box.* Cambridge: University of Cambridge, School of Education.

Barrs, M., Ellis, S., Hester, H. and Thomas, A. (1988) *The Primary Language Record.* London: CLPE.

Black, P., Harrison, C., Lee, C., Marshall, B. and Wiliam, D. (2003) *Assessment for Learning.* Maidenhead: Open University Press.

Browne, A. (1998) *Teaching Reading in the Early Years.* London: Paul Chapman.

Clarke, S. (2004) *Unlocking Formative Assessment.* London: Hodder & Stoughton.

Classroom Discourse Project, available at: www.griffith.edu.au/schools/cls/clearinghouse/1998classroom/cal.pdf

DfEE (1998) *The National Literacy Strategy: Framework for Teaching.* London: HMSO.

DfEE (2000) *English in the National Curriculum.* London: HMSO.

DfES (2003) *Speaking, Listening, Learning: Working with Children in Key Stages 1 and 2.* London: QCA.

DfES (2005) *Assessment and Reporting Arrangements.* London: QCA.

Drummond, M.J. (2003) *Assessing Children's Learning.* London: David Fulton Publishers.

Fisher, R. (1998) 'Thinking about thinking: developing metacognition in children', *Early Child Development and Care*, 141: 1–13.

Hall, K. and Burke, W.M. (2003) *Making Formative Assessment Work.* Maidenhead: Open University Press.

Halliday, M.A.K. (1978) *Language and Social Semiotic: The Social Interpretation of Language and Meaning.* London: Heinemann.

Koshy, V. and Mitchell, C. (1993) *Effective Assessment.* London: Hodder & Stoughton.

Mercer, N. (2000) *Words and Minds: How We Use Language to Think Together.* London: Routledge.

Norman, K. (1992) *Thinking Voices: The Work of the National Oracy Project.* London: Hodder and Stoughton.

Pollard, A. *et al.* (2005) *Reflective Teaching: Evidence Informed Professional Practice.* London: Continuum.

QCA 'Assessment for Learning' available at: http://www.qca.org.uk/10009.html

QCA (1999) *Target Setting and Assessment in the National Literacy Strategy.* London: QCA.

Raison, G. (1996) *First Steps.* Harlow: Longman.

Raison, G. *et al.* (1996) *Oral Development Continuum.* Harlow: Longman.

Sadler, R. (1998) 'Formative assessment and the design of instructional systems', *Instructional Science*, 18: 119–44.

Torrance, H. and Pryor, J. (2002) *Investigating Formative Assessment.* Maidenhead: Open University Press.

Vygotsky, L.S. (1978) *Mind in Society: The Development of Higher Psychological Processes.* Cambridge, MA: Harvard University Press.

Scaffolding learning: speaking, listening and EAL pupils

Ruth Lewis

For teachers who have never taught pupils with English as an Additional Language (EAL), it can be daunting to be in a classroom where the majority of pupils are bilingual learners. The challenge for the teacher is to determine what a child who ostensibly 'doesn't speak a word' can actually understand. Although some children may seem to speak little or no English, on further investigation they may display a range of linguistic competences. Their level of spoken English could range from full native competence, be limited to social communication only, or be in the very early stages of learning English. They may come from a range of linguistic and cultural backgrounds. They could have been born in the UK, arrived a couple of years ago or just last week. The aim of this chapter is to locate the teaching of these children within an historical context but essentially to provide classroom teachers with practical strategies for teaching EAL pupils

Historical context and background to EAL teaching

Towards the end of the 1960s the government became aware that there were an increasing number of pupils arriving in schools speaking little or no English. In an effort to provide support for these children, specialist training courses for teachers were set up in large urban areas such as Leeds, Liverpool and London. The funding, from the Home Office, was referred to as Section 11. The term used to classify these children was 'immigrants' and the specialist teaching as English as a Second Language (ESL or E2L). As a result, ESL pupils were often taught in separate classrooms from their peers for at least part of the week and in some cases attended specialist units full-time until they were considered able to cope in the mainstream classroom. Often there was no attempt made to link the pupils' learning of English to the mainstream curriculum. This would have been very difficult, as the groups of ESL pupils were often from different age groups and there was, at this time, no National Curriculum. Many of the strategies and materials were based on teaching English as a Foreign Language or resources developed for pupils with learning difficulties.

During the 1970s and 1980s concern grew among educators, parents and some politicians that the pupils of ethnic minority families were often receiving a second-rate education and that withdrawal of pupils from the classroom was not actually providing the benefit that was originally intended. Parents complained that teachers ignored their children's home culture and language so that the pupils felt inferior and lacked confidence in the classroom. It was also discovered that in some LEAs, Section 11 funding was being misused. It was increasingly felt that withdrawing pupils from the classroom on the basis of what could appear to be skin colour rather than language need was a form of racism.

Consequently, policies and practice began to change. Specialist English language teachers developed partnership teaching strategies with class teachers. In the best examples of practice, two teachers working together would provide good role models for the pupils and develop interactive communication strategies across all areas of the curriculum. In this way, bilingual learners could be supported in the classroom alongside their peer group and also gain access to the National Curriculum. In some LEAs community language staff were employed to help with translation and interpreting for young pupils new to school or new arrivals who arrived as midterm admissions. They were also able to help schools to communicate with parents who had only a little English.

During the 1990s the descriptive term 'English as an Additional Language' (EAL) was introduced into government literature. It is now used for pupils who are in the process of learning English on entry to school. There are often more than two languages spoken or written in these pupils' home backgrounds, making the description 'English as a second language' (ESL or E2L) not necessarily an accurate one. The term EAL is intended to recognise that in learning English, not as an option but as the prime language of instruction, pupils are adding to their existing linguistic skills.

In 1999 the funding of EAL teaching was transferred from the Home Office to the Department for Education and Skills and is currently distributed to LEAs via the Standards Fund. It is now known as the Ethnic Minorities Achievement Grant (EMAG). There have been numerous government initiatives that have affected the way that education for EAL pupils is delivered in the classroom. The inclusion model of guidance for EAL pupils relating to the Primary National Strategy has meant that the emphasis has changed dramatically. EAL pupils are expected to achieve national targets alongside their peers. The emphasis is on whole-class teaching with appropriate differentiated tasks for individuals or groups. There are extra teaching assistants in the classroom and various accelerated learning programmes, from after school homework clubs, to targeted extra NLS sessions for those that have not met the national literacy targets.

In 2003, the DfES announced the first national strategy to tackle underachievement among minority ethnic pupils. The *Aiming High*[1] strategy includes targeted activities on narrowing achievement gaps and is currently funding Primary National Strategy EAL programmes in 21 LEAs. LEA consultants work with schools to equip mainstream staff to meet the needs of bilingual pupils.

Recent statistics collected from UK primary schools have shown that as a result of the strong emphasis on reading and writing in the National Literacy Strategy, there is now concern that primary age pupils lack effective speaking and listening skills. Consequently, new guidelines on speaking and listening[2] with schemes of work have been produced by the DfES.

The development of speaking and listening skills in their new language of learning is very important for all bilingual learners. Sometimes, teachers feel pressurised into concentrating on reading and writing skills before a pupil has had the opportunity to practise their newly learnt vocabulary. A key feature of schools where bilingual learners achieve well is that careful attention is given to oral language development. Consequently, the DfES, as part of its EAL pilot, is in the process of developing specific sessions for additional language acquisition which focus on speaking and listening. These are not aimed at beginners to English but to those pupils who have had a considerable exposure to English in an educational environment.

Multilingual approaches in the classroom

Bilingual learners are all those children who have access to more than one language at home or at school. It does not necessarily imply that they have full fluency in both or all languages. Offering bilingual children the opportunity to continue to use their first language alongside English will support their overall academic achievement and provide them with the opportunity to engage in cognitively demanding tasks. Monolingual teachers often ask how they can provide this support. 'The Multilingual Resources for Children Project' has produced a useful book on the subject: *Building Bridges: Multilingual Resources for Children.*[3] This includes a section on creating the right ethos and resources for speaking and listening.

Current government thinking recognises that bilingualism is an asset. It encourages teachers to show pupils that their languages are valued through some simple strategies:

- Explicit celebration of linguistic diversity throughout the school through multilingual displays.

- Learning songs and rhymes in other languages.
- Encouraging bilingual staff and parents to participate in dual language storytelling.
- Encouraging the social use of all languages in the school by adults and children.
- Pre-teaching of new concepts in first language to provide a supportive context for EAL pupils at different stages of learning English.

Supporting new arrivals

The diverse needs of EAL pupils

When planning speaking and listening opportunities for EAL pupils, it is important for teaching staff to gain as much knowledge as possible about individual children. Efforts should be made to find out how much English is already understood by a new arrival. This can be observed in the way that a pupil responds to individual and class instructions and their interaction with other pupils in the classroom. The QCA document *A Language in Common*[4] gives some guidance on EAL pupils' stages of language development. In April 2005 the Department for Education and Skills issued guidance on the assessment of pupils learning English as an additional language where they advise schools to use the QCA fluency scales for summative assessment.

Creating a welcoming environment

It is important at an early stage to welcome a new arrival in a friendly manner and encourage the class to do the same. If there is a pupil in the class who speaks the same language, it can certainly encourage the recent arrival to communicate and set them at their ease. In any case, it is important to ensure that some members of the class are willing to be 'buddies' and introduce the new arrival to the routines of the classroom and school. It is helpful to remind the class to speak in a normal tone of voice to them and avoid baby talk. Learning how to pronounce the new pupil's name correctly and teaching it to the class, will help the new child's settling in process. It is also useful if a few words or phrases, such as greetings, of the new pupil's home language are taught to the class and used at appropriate times.

The classroom should reflect a variety of other cultures, in terms of pictures, posters, books and artefacts. For instance, many schools and classrooms have 'Welcome' posters in a range of languages in their entrance halls or on the classroom door. Some classrooms have a globe or world map available for children to discuss and label. The most important thing about helping children to acquire a new language for learning is to provide them with a secure and welcoming environment where they will develop the confidence to use talk as a natural part of their learning across the curriculum.

Background information

Gathering background information on any new arrival enables the teacher to take into account the particular needs of the child. This may especially be the case if, for example, children from refugee or asylum seeker families may have very particular needs which demand sensitive treatment. If the parents and child speak limited English, an interpreter can help to build a relationship between home and school. In this way school expectations can be explained and background information can be obtained. Sometimes, this specific information may already be on the school registration form. If not, then a checklist might include:

- date of birth;
- correct pronunciation of name/preferred name;
- languages spoken/understood and preferred language;
- literacy in languages other than English;
- competency in English;
- prior experience of formal learning or lack of it;
- prior life experiences. This might include life in a refugee camp, loss of a close relative, living in a war-torn country or other traumatic experiences;
- parental attitudes and expectations;
- information about siblings, relatives and friends living locally;
- religion and dietary needs;
- housing arrangements;
- medical history.

It is important not to make assumptions about a new pupil and either underestimate their capabilities or overestimate their understanding. Children may initially suffer from culture shock and will just need a little time to settle into their new surroundings before they begin to speak in English. They may have been to an English-medium school in Asia or Africa and have difficulty in 'tuning in' to different pronunciation. They may also have difficulty in making their spoken English understood, which can be distressing for them. Some children will seem as though they can understand every word and nod their heads and say 'Yes' to everything, even though they have a very limited understanding of English and as a consequence may be overlooked in a busy classroom. On the other hand pupils may be wrongly identified as having special educational needs when it is their level of understanding of the English language that needs identifying and supporting.

Some refugee/asylum seeker children may not have been to school before and will need a lot of support with handwriting skills, oral skills, classroom and playground behaviour, to name but a few. In cases where they have been witnesses to particularly traumatic events, they may need a lot of emotional support and understanding. As one parent said to his child's teacher, 'Never mind his SATs results. I long for the day when my son will learn to smile again.'

Sometimes teachers forget that their new arrival already speaks at least one other language. Many EAL pupils already speak several languages on their arrival in the UK, which is why we refer to our pupils as learning English as an additional language. It is therefore incorrect to say 'She doesn't speak a word!' This implies that the pupil has arrived in the classroom without any prior knowledge or experience or basic concepts in any language, even their own. It is through the skill of the teacher that the child will be able to transfer their existing experiences into the new language of learning.

Silent time

It is easy to forget that it is exhausting learning a new language and pupils will be very tired during their first few weeks. Many pupils will stay silent for weeks or even months before they will speak in class, even to answer the register. It is very important for them that they are given the chance to assimilate what they are hearing. This can feel very frustrating for teachers especially when they see that the child can understand them and perhaps talks to friends in the playground. The pupil's attitude will depend partly on their personality. An extrovert child will often be desperate to communicate and young children, in particular, may talk in their home language in an effort to make themselves understood. A shy or reserved child may take much longer to feel confident enough to speak in class or to adults. While it is important to encourage pupils to speak whenever there is an opportunity, it is usually counter-productive to try to force them or put them under any pressure. Some children are perfectionists and will not speak until they feel confident enough to talk in whole phrases or sentences and as accurately as possible.

CASE STUDY

A Chinese girl who had been in school in England for two years and could follow complex instructions easily was refusing to speak to her teacher. She would mouth the words in her reading book but it was impossible to hear whether her intonation or pronunciation was correct. Her classmates all said, 'She doesn't speak, Miss.' Her parents, who spoke English well, were very concerned about her. A mother tongue assessment in Cantonese showed that she was performing at a very high level for her age. After working in a small group where we used role play and choral work to support the understanding of stories from Literacy Hour, she suddenly began to speak aloud when given the role of a cat. This play was then performed in front of the whole class and when she made her contribution her classmates were astounded and clapped and said, 'She can speak!' She received much praise from the teacher and from then on made regular contributions to classroom discussion and her spoken language in English was quite accurate and continued to develop normally.

Each child needs a different approach. Some pupils who have come from a different education system may have been taught that it is very rude to look the teacher directly in the face and will look away or hang their heads when spoken to. This illustrates that teachers need to gather as much information as possible about children and their different backgrounds. This can be taken for rudeness and children may be mistakenly punished for this. If pupils take a very long time to start talking in English, it is worth having a mother tongue assessment, if possible, to see if they are speaking fluently in their own language.

The teacher's role

Organising the classroom

In any primary classroom there are certain *key principles* which will help to support EAL pupils in their language development. It is important that all pupils and adults working in your classroom respect purposeful talk as a learning tool. It is worth spending some time setting criteria with the class to identify what are the qualities of being a good listener and a good speaker. If all the pupils in your class are using speaking and listening rules, then it is much easier for EAL pupils to become active listeners and speakers themselves. These rules could include the following:

Listening

- I sit quietly and look at the person who is talking.
- I listen carefully to make sure that I can understand.
- I wait until the other person has finished talking before I talk.
- I ask a question if I don't understand.

Speaking

- I make sure that people are ready to listen.
- I look at the people I am talking to.
- I speak clearly.
- I let others join in.

By using the above rules and praising pupils when they fulfil them, high standards can be set in an area of learning which children, their parents and sometimes other adults do not always value. In some schools where there is a whole-school policy on speaking and listening, you will find teachers using badges, stickers and certificates to encourage 'good listening'.

Teacher talk

The teacher plays a vital role both in modelling language for the EAL child and in speaking in a way which is accessible. The following suggestions may be shared with teaching assistants, parent volunteers, students or any other classroom helpers.

- Be consistent in classroom routines and language. For example, ringing a bell, clapping your hands and holding up your hand as a signal for silence will create confusion. It is best to use one agreed signal.
- Give instructions that are direct and unambiguous, e.g. 'Come and sit on the carpet' followed by 'Can I see everyone sitting on the mat, please' is going to confuse EAL pupils, particularly those who are in the early stages of learning English.
- Avoid giving too many instructions at once. An EAL pupil will find it difficult to retain a lot of information at once and may appear not to be listening. Often they will respond either to the first thing that the teacher said or the last thing because they are unable to manage more than one instruction at a time. Some teachers find 'prompt boards' with visual messages/reminders displayed around the classroom very useful.
- Paraphrase and recast teacher-talk to promote understanding.
- Allow EAL pupils more thinking time when they are asked direct questions. Using talking partners will help pupils to rehearse their answers before answering in front of the whole class.
- In questioning use clarification checks. For example, 'Can you tell me *three* things that I just said?' and 'Check first with your partner', rather than, 'Do you understand?'

- Tell pupils in advance that you will be asking them questions in a moment about the following information.

- Differentiate your questioning. Ask questions of bilingual learners that are appropriate to their level of English language proficiency. For example, beginners might be asked 'What' and 'Where' questions, while more advanced EAL learners may manage more open questions beginning with 'How' or 'Why'.

- Model procedures and texts in preparation for activities and writing tasks. Ensure that they know *how* to do a task as well as *what* to do.

- Use 'hands-on' practical activities to support the use of new language. For example, cookery, science and craft activities work well when organised into groups that will provide effective 'good quality' language.

- Encourage active oral participation. Elicit lengthier responses to questions, giving prompts where necessary. Allow for pupil initiation of questions and praise pupils for good examples of questioning. Encourage the use of new content-related language in pupil talk.

Opportunities to practise and rehearse a new language

Accessing language across the curriculum

It is worth remembering that every lesson can be a language lesson and that language needs to be taught across the whole curriculum. Every subject area has specific characteristics. For example, PE provides opportunities for pupils to follow and give instructions, and to learn the names of different parts of the body and its actions in context: 'Throw the ball to your partner', or 'Curl up, tuck your heads in and do a forward roll.'

Science involves the language of instructions, describing a process and reporting back.

'1. Put some cold water in the bowl.'   'First we put cold water in the bowl.'
'2. Add one teaspoon of salt.'   'Then we added one teaspoon of salt.'

History creates opportunities for thinking chronologically, and asking questions and retelling past events.

'When was Mary Seacole born?'
'She was born in Jamaica in 1805.'

Gibbons[5] warns against 'restricting children to using set phrases and predetermined language within a particular learning activity'. She advises that 'an important concept in language acquisition is the notion of the learner needing to hear models of language which are *comprehensible* but also *beyond what the learners are able to produce themselves*'. In order to plan effective speaking and listening activities across all areas of the curriculum, it is advisable to become aware of the range of language functions that are used in every primary classroom every day. Gibbons provides a useful list of the more common functions of language including planning and predicting, explaining, hypothesising, comparing, describing, etc. All these language functions can be found embedded in the National Curriculum.

Strategies and resources

The following strategies and resources have proved useful in developing communication skills in the classroom for all pupils but particularly EAL learners. They can be appropriately adapted for all primary age groups. Where possible, examples have been given for both Key Stage 1 and Key Stage 2. Some of them would be appropriate as group literacy activities during Literacy Hour where speaking and listening can be a focus. This would be particularly useful when other adults are available to lead a group. While emphasising the importance of speaking and listening the strategies are part of an integrated approach to developing all four literacy skills. By focusing on ways that teachers can employ to 'scaffold' language and learning in the content areas of the curriculum, these strategies allow non-specialist EAL teachers to meet the challenge of catering for the needs of linguistically diverse students.

Home-made books are easy and inexpensive to make and are very useful for the bilingual child learning English. They could be text-free, or offer limited text or could include the pupil's own language. They provide supportive language structures, stimulate speech and offer restricted vocabulary (word banks), which is helpful for children at this stage. In addition, the language of making books is very important and should be taught:

- instructions such as cut, stick and copy;
- position words such as top, bottom cover, pages (numbers);
- book words such as front, back, cover, pages, contents, index.

Children can 'read' all these books to a variety of audiences and use them for reading practice.

Storytelling with props/role play can be used even with new arrivals because they provide a context for language learning. They are also visual, dramatic and fun. The kinds of stories that best meet the needs of EAL beginners are:

- those with repetitive or predictable refrains or storylines;
- those whose language structure and vocabulary are natural;

- those clearly supported by good illustrations;
- those that span cultural and age boundaries, e.g. traditional tales.

Activities that will support pupils' access to the story and encourage them to name the characters, complete the dialogue and begin to retell the story could include the following:

- story props, e.g. puppets or magnet board figures to rehearse and familiarise the language of the story;
- information or structure grids – to help clarify and organise information, rehearse spoken language and support the creation of sentences;
- story grids for picture sequencing with matching sentences with a repeating structure;
- riddles;
- comic strips to retell the story;
- story maps to draw and retell the story;
- T charts for classifying, e.g. can/can't; like/don't like;
- true/false tick charts;
- Language Master (magnetic cards for listening and recording short audio clips);
- songs and rhymes that will reinforce the language of the chosen story;
- role play – acting out the story with pupils as the characters and with short scripted parts of a repetitive dialogue;
- Small People and/or Shoebox Theatres to act out the scenes from a story (Key Stage 2 pupils may find this a helpful strategy when asked to create stories with alternative endings);
- Talk Box – screen off an area of the classroom or build a large, decorated, box with a tape recorder inside where individual pupils can be encouraged to record stories, poems, songs or messages in English or other languages for their teacher or friends to listen to at a later date. The privacy and regular use of this system encourage reserved pupils to risk making errors and learn to correct their speech themselves. Teachers will also have evidence of progression if the audio tapes are dated.

Songs, rhymes and poetry

Songs, rhymes and poetry for young learners of English should be a natural part of everyday life in the classroom. Many young bilingual learners will mouth the words of songs and rhymes and join in the actions long before they will sing them aloud. Being part of a group who will carry on singing even if they forget the words will give them the confidence to develop a repertoire of songs and rhymes often before they can speak in full sentences. Obviously, choosing songs which have a repetitive refrain or chorus is always helpful. Some teachers with large numbers of EAL pupils in their class find making props to match the rhymes adds a three-dimensional aspect which aids understanding for children who are not sure what five currant buns look or taste like, for example. Bilingual parents can also be encouraged to teach songs from their own cultural background in school.

When selecting poems, it is important to use those from a range of cultural backgrounds as well as with different features. Such poetry can be of great benefit to bilingual learners. It offers succinct texts and the use of repetition. It can give opportunities to read and repeat the same piece of text and in addition the rhythm and rhyme can give a feel for the new language. Pupils can also benefit from sharing poems through performance. A class can be divided into groups to work on either the same piece of text or different poems depending on the experience of the pupils. It is important that the groups contain at least one experienced reader and the bilingual learners who are in the early stages of learning English are not all in one group. By choosing appropriate poems that can offer repetitive refrains or simple structures, all the children can participate and bilingual learners will be provided with scaffolds by these approaches.

Using key visuals

For many years specialist EAL staff have been using a variety of grids and charts to scaffold pupils' thinking and ability to express their thoughts verbally, in all areas of the curriculum (Figure 9.1).

Children's language can be supported further by providing them with sentence supports. These are structures which will enable them to express their thoughts and ideas using language and sentence constructions which are not part of their normal everyday speech (Figure 9.2).

Children learning EAL will usually acquire basic conversational English relatively quickly. However, the acquisition of academic English required to access the curriculum takes much longer. In this chapter, a range of strategies have been discussed which will help EAL learners accelerate their language development. The most important element of all is the teacher's role in building a strong relationship with bilingual learners. This is a process which is both stimulating and rewarding. Cummins[6] summarises this succinctly through the words of a pupil: 'Our classroom was full of human knowledge. We had a teacher who believed in us…he didn't hide our power, he advertised it.' Therein lies the challenge for teachers working within a linguistically rich and diverse society.

Learning Prompts – Key Visuals

Learning prompts help EAL pupils to articulate their ideas and provide a 'frame' for a particular form of language structure. They may include highlighted key vocabulary diagrams and/or other scaffolds to learning in the form of key visuals. They help the pupils to organise their thinking around the focused activity and facilitate the recall of key words and phrases rather than large chunks of text.

- T CHARTS

hot	cold

These are useful for teaching concept language, e.g. big/small, hot/cold, like/don't like. Pictures can be discussed and sorted into appropriate categories, labelled and then used as a basis for writing repeating sentences.

These charts can be further divided to include more categories

paper	glass	tin	cardboard

- STRUCTURED SEQUENCE CHARTS

These are useful for follow-up to practical activities and storytelling, e.g. cooking, science.

1 saucepan	2 noodles
3 8 mins cook	4 eat

1. First we boiled the water.
2. Next we put the noodles in the saucepan.
3. Then we cooked the noodles for 8 minutes.
4. Lastly we put soy sauce on and ate them.

FIGURE 9.1 Learning prompts

Sentence Supports

Choose a feature from the text

There was a good example of ....

in the .... **text when the writer said**

....

Find the thesis of the text

In the .... **text, it was clear that the writer**

believed ....

Find the arguments of the text

In the .... **text, the writer wants the reader to**...........

....

Looking for patterns

The writer did not use .... **in the**

.... **text because** ....

....

FIGURE 9.2 Year 6 sentence supports

Notes

1. DfES (2003a).
2. DfES (2003b).
3. Baker (1995).
4. QCA (2000).
5. Gibbons (1991).
6. Cummins (1996).

References and further reading

Baker, C. (ed.) (1995) *Building Bridges: Multilingual Resources for Children.* Clevedon: Multilingual Matters Ltd.

Brooker, L. (2002) *Starting School: Young Children Learning Cultures.* Buckingham: Open University Press.

Cummins, J. (1996) *Negotiating Identities: Education for Empowerment in a Diverse Society.* Ontario: California Association for Bilingual Education.

DfES (2003a) *Aiming High: Guidance on the Assessment of Pupils Learning English as an Additional Language.* Nottingham: DfES.

DfES (2003b) *Speaking, Listening, Learning: Working with Children in Key Stages 1 and 2.* London: QCA.

Gibbons, P. (1991) *Learning to Learn in a Second Language.* Newtown, Australia: Primary English Teaching Association.

Gregory, E. (1996) *Making Sense of a New World.* London: Paul Chapman Publishing.

Gregory, E. (1997) *One Child, Many Worlds: Early Learning in Multicultural Communities.* London: David Fulton Publishers.

Hall, C. *et al.* (2004) *EAL at Key Stage 1: Framework for Early Stages.* London: Hounslow Language Service.

Hall, D. (1995) *Assessing the Needs of Bilingual Pupils: Living in Two Languages.* London: David Fulton Publishers.

Harvey, A. (2003) *EAL Across the Curriculum: Key Visuals.* London: Hounslow Language Service.

Lewis, R. *et al.* (2005) *Access and Inclusion: Beginners in English in Primary Schools.* London: Hounslow Language Service.

Melhuish, J. (2003) *Quality Teaching in a Multicultural Setting: Persuasive Writing in Year 6* (video and training materials) London: Lifelong Learning and Cultural Service.

QCA (2000) *A Language in Common.* London: QCA.

Resources

EAL and language materials

Hounslow Language Service website (www.ealinhounslow.org.uk) includes access to the full publications catalogue of EAL and multilingual resources.

Language Master
Drake Educational Associates
St Fagans Road
Cardiff
tel. 029 2056 0333

The Refugee Council Head Office
240–250 Ferndale Road
London SW9 8BB
tel. 020 7346 6700

Multicultural and multilingual resources list

Hope Education: 08451 20 20 55 www.hope-education.co.uk
Mantra Lingua: 020 8445 5123 www.mantralingua.com
Milet Publishing Ltd: 020 7603 5477 www.milet.com
NES Arnold: 0845 120 4525 www.nesarnold.co.uk
The Festival Shop Ltd: email: info@festivalshop.co.uk

Computer software

Clicker 5 is a powerful writing and multimedia tool that combines a talking word processor with picture grids.
First Talking Stories (Oxford Reading Tree).
Multilingual Talking Books (Hounslow Language Service).
My First Dictionary, Ages 3–7 (Dorling Kindersley).

Emphasising the 'C' in ICT: speaking, listening and communication

Yota Dimitriadi, Pamela Hodson and Geeta Ludhra

Joti, Harry, Isobel and Gurdeep, four Year 2 pupils, were filming a sequence of shots using a digital video camera to provide instructions for visitors to help them navigate around their school. Joti and Harry were being guided by Gurdeep on where to stand. Gurdeep stood back and evaluated the image she could see through her camera: 'Stand closer and look this way.'

'If you pan left and right slowly, you'll be able to see all of the playground,' suggested Isobel and they all agreed. As the filming started, Isobel counted in the presenters who introduced themselves, welcomed potential visitors to their school and gave clear explanations and instructions on routes around the school.

In this extended activity, ICT, in the form of digital video, offered the children opportunities to work in role, engage in real-time situations which promoted teamwork and involved them in choosing an appropriate genre to address purpose and audience.[1] Digital film-making is an example of the multimedia opportunities offered by the availability of more inexpensive and easy to use digital cameras, camcorders and video editing software. The integration of digital video is becoming increasingly popular not only as a teaching and learning resource, but its potential for the development of a range of social skills, including problem-solving,[2] communication, negotiation (Becta 2003b) and self-perception (Becta and BFI 2002) has also been recognised. As film-makers, children are encouraged to develop a voice in the creative process, to explore ideas and reflect upon their decisions and to work effectively as part of a group.[3]

This chapter explores the opportunities that ICT offers for communication in the primary classroom and innovations in teachers' practice. The term ICT is used to encompass technological resources that can assist, enrich or replace current practices and support interaction and communication. In this context, computer-related activities will be considered, together with the use of other digital resources like cameras or programmable toys.

What follows is a discussion of how ICT can enrich speaking and listening activities and factors that need to be considered when organising ICT-related tasks with children. The key role of ICT and children's spoken language skills will be contextualised within the current National Curriculum, the Primary Strategy and key initiatives such as *Speaking, Listening, Learning* (DfES 2003c) and *Excellence and Enjoyment* (DfES 2003b). The terms 'communication' and 'interaction' will also be used to address inclusive uses of technology. This is particularly important as the term 'speaking and listening' can point out to verbal exchanges in which some children with special educational needs or disabilities may not be able to participate fully. It also allows us to view the contribution of ICT to receptive and expressive interactions in a more holistic way, something which will be relevant in the case of children with English as an additional language (EAL). In this context, 'speaking and listening' will be used to include expressive and receptive communication skills which may be observed in verbal and non-verbal utterances. This approach is concomitant with the Speaking, Listening and Learning exemplification materials produced to support children with special educational needs.

Other key areas for consideration will be the kinds of speaking and listening that a range of ICT resources promote and how these opportunities for communication can be effectively embedded in the curriculum. Specific packages will not be evaluated, but rather, families of programs and peripherals along with their potential to support communication and group work will be discussed.

The current context

Teachers are now being actively encouraged to adopt a more flexible approach to teaching literacy and using ICT effectively in the classroom can have positive effects in enabling teachers to re-evaluate how they teach English. Becta (2003b) identifies research[4] whereby ICT allows for opportunities in which teacher direction is reduced and children's control and self-regulation are increased.

Promoting involvement of all children and young people and especially the most vulnerable ones in society also comes as a direct outcome of government policy within the children's agenda delineated in 'Every Child Matters' (DfES 2003a),[5] something which can support the development of more empowering practices in terms of children's participation within the curriculum. New technologies, as cultural commodities, can facilitate children's active involvement in developing a voice about themselves and the world around them.

In terms of speaking and listening, ICT can enable children to enrich a range of social learning skills such as communication, negotiation, decision-making and problem-solving[6] in a meaningful context. These skills are consistent with the requirements of the primary ICT curriculum in which the children are expected to develop skills, knowledge and understanding of appropriate uses of technology, coined under the term 'ICT capability' (DfEE 1999: 99). The children's ICT explorations need to demonstrate 'a conceptual understanding of the ways in which information is organised, accessed, presented and communicated with these technologies' (Sharp *et al.* 2002: 2).

The four strands of the Programmes of Study for ICT in the National Curriculum for England highlight the importance of speaking and listening as they suggest that ICT activities need to be collaborative and investigative. When children are engaged in 'exchanging and sharing information', 'developing ideas and making things happen', 'finding things out' or 'reviewing, modifying and evaluating work as it progresses', they are expected to develop communicative skills by participating in group activities and justifying their individual choices. In the wider context that the breadth of study covers, the children are also encouraged to explore and talk about uses of ICT within and outside the school. The ICT curriculum emphasises the importance of children developing skills progressively to describe, present and evaluate their work by taking into consideration purpose, relevance and appropriateness for their audience.

Communication is a key area in the Foundation Stage as well. Young children are involved in exploring and describing the world and themselves to peers and adults. The opportunities for ICT are embedded within all six Early Learning Goals and can take the form of playful activities in which a range of resources can be used: from metal detectors to programmable toys and digital cameras.

Supporting engagement and interaction

Interaction is embedded within all ICT applications. Talking word processors, symbol processing programs or personal aids such as voice activated software provide users opportunities to learn and exchange information by employing diverse ways of communication like their voice, pictures and symbols. Table 10.1 indicates how ICT can involve children in a range of speaking and listening contexts and activities. Organisations like NESTA Futurelab (http://www.nestafuturelab.org) support creative uses of new technologies and also evaluate current approaches and use of digital resources. The 'Teem' (Teachers Evaluating Educational Multimedia) website (http://www.teem.org.uk) offers evaluations of educational software and websites.

Table 10.1 How ICT can involve children in a range of speaking and listening contexts and activities

Communicative functions	Activities and resources
Collaboration	working together on game-format activities, researching topics on the web to produce presentations, working in groups to develop digital videos, music and other multimedia work
Communication	WWW, email, Talking Books, voice activated software, symbol processing software, presentation packages, storyboarding programs, desktop publishing software, digital cameras, art packages, video conferencing, talking word processors, PC tablets
Evaluation	analysing media work, selecting relevant and appropriate information from the web and justifying their choices
Reflection	programmable toys, webquests, control technology, developing and interpreting graphs

These new technologies have started shaping speaking, listening and writing activities offering 'more fluid and informal forms of communication which in turn will influence decisions about the speaking and listening curriculum', as Eve Bearne argues.[7] However, she continues, 'it is important to be able to distinguish between shifts in practices brought about by digital technology and fundamental changes in forms of language'.

What is becoming more and more challenging is a change of discourse conventions that accompanies the use of communication technologies. For instance, mobile phones have become popular media in the lives of many young people who choose them as favourite ways of keeping in touch with their local social networks.[8] Emoticons or abbreviations, usual features in texting, are considered as purposeful and legitimate elements of interactions and are used to indicate ideas, actions and pauses, all integral attributes of dialogical exchanges.

These functional uses of new technologies can often blend boundaries between formal and informal communications and settings creating some continuities between prior experiences and knowledge for the 'digital natives' as children are sometimes described in the literature.[9] At the same time though they can create some discontinuities when their use is not supported by careful consideration of how they can provide accessible and purposeful ways of extending all children's knowledge, skills and capabilities.

The importance of planning for diversity is also highlighted by the principles of the inclusion statement of the National Curriculum. The statement recognises the importance of providing access for all pupils to overcome barriers to learning, which in terms of ICT will include software and hardware. However, it also points out the importance of adapting our teaching styles and setting suitable learning challenges to support all learners.

ICT enhancing current practices

ICT does not aim to replace successful speaking and listening activities that are better presented without the use of technology but enhance current practices in new and innovative ways. For instance, the Internet is a research and learning resource that can support active participation as well as synchronous or asynchronous discussion of ideas. Consider the use of emailing, which allows users to communicate with people from all over the world or the use of video-conferencing applications that can provide children with a vast range of audiences for speaking and listening activities. However, some Internet uses, such as online chats, may need careful consideration due to their unmediated nature.[10] Exposure to risks and unsuitable online materials is one of the current concerns regarding Internet uses for schools. Becta with the DfES and Ultralab (2003b) have produced a teaching pack with suggested activities and hosted an interactive site aimed for Key Stage 2 pupils to support awareness about safe Internet uses.

The use of VLEs (Virtual Learning Environments), which provide activities in password-protected areas on the web, become more and more popular in educational settings. Some primary schools use part of their e-learning credits to purchase access to content-rich online resources which include video clips, worksheets, interactive tasks for cross-curricular activities. In terms of speaking and listening what the teacher needs to ensure is that these online activities are supported by opportunities for discussion among the children during the tasks as well as away from the screen. As Mercer and Wegerif[11] suggest, the computer can play the role of prompting and sustaining children's use of 'exploratory talk' framing the discussion and directing it towards specific outcomes. What they define as 'exploratory talk' is a communicative process for reasoning through talk in the context of some specific joint activity. Children working on a computer simulation, finding information on a webpage or an informational CD-ROM or developing a newspaper article together can discuss and negotiate the development of their thinking.

In this context, ICT becomes a concrete medium for the children to negotiate or describe ideas. In a Reception class the children were learning about healthy eating. They had to use a drawing package to draw some 'healthy' food and then describe their drawing to the adult who was supporting them. The particular activity would have been more demanding on paper as it would have been more difficult for them to edit the pictures they drew. It also gave the adult assistant the opportunity to assess the children's IT skills (for instance, mouse control, hand–eye co-ordination) and discuss the use of colour, shape and the notions of 'background' and 'foreground' as they were developing their drawings. At the same time in the class next door the children were working in pairs taking pictures of each other after they had put their overcoats, hats and gloves on. The activity was based on sequencing. The pictures were then saved in their individual portfolios and formed part of their Profiles.

CASE STUDY 1

A group of 18 higher ability Year 6 pupils were studying the poetic features and structures of the witches' chant, 'Hubble Bubble' from William Shakespeare's tragedy *Macbeth*. Through their study of well-known poets, they were developing their oral performance skills. A simple piece of technology – the cassette recorder – provided a running record of the performances and development processes up to the finished, final product. The tape recorder allowed the children to hear themselves develop as confident performers over four stages of recording (mirroring the drafting and editing process in the written form).

> The tape recorder helped me listen to my voice and I realised that my voice wasn't projecting as well as others in my team. Me and my team worked really hard to get it right after draft one. Draft four was a lot better – I actually sounded quite scary.
>
> (Rupinder, age 10)

The use of the cassette recorder offered the children a valuable auditory opportunity to focus on speaking and listening skills as two distinct, yet closely related skills. Speaking and listening skills need to be explicitly taught, rehearsed and modelled by the class teacher, especially in a bilingual environment where the models at home are often in their mother tongue. Classic poetry like Shakespeare can be made accessible and brought to life for bilingual learners if they are provided with multi-sensory opportunities to 'feel' the rhythm and pattern of such classic poems and rehearse them by heart (like a favourite piece of music).

Most of the children in the class were advanced bilingual learners and confident speakers of their mother tongue. They were fluent users of English, yet slightly reserved about performing orally in a dramatic Shakespearian style. Opportunities were given for children to learn through personal reflection and constructive criticism. Through this activity, they were enabled to critically evaluate their own vocal performance skills within a small group.

The children became both the audience and critics for their own work – the simple tape recorder made this possible. The different groups in the class worked together as a team to put together a complete performance. Positive criticism was accepted and discussed where disagreements arose.

Draft one of the oral performance was recorded and the children were provided with short 'time-out' discussion opportunities to discuss and evaluate ways forward. The discussions focused around areas like:

- the use of simple vocal and sound effects;
- the variation of pitch at different lines;
- voice projection skills/volume;
- 'best fit' parts for the line/s.

Some children were given different speaking parts after listening to draft one. Children discussed whose voices should be used together in the performance of particular lines, the use of volume and greater emphasis on certain words for effect (close links with musical elements of texture and timbre).

The children were actively engaged in developing vital language skills in a process of:

- oral performance;
- listening and reflecting;
- evaluating;
- organising different roles;
- discussing, exploring and investigating different approaches.

Without the use of cassette recorder technology such enrichment, depth and reflection would not have been possible.

> My team knew what we had to do to make it better. Draft 1 wasn't very good at all, we did not create witchy voices or use expression well. You could hardly hear some of our voices. By draft 4 we performed the voices and rhyme patterns spot on. I think we performed well because in our discussions we chose lines that we were confident with.
>
> (Lloyd, age 11)

Storyboarding software also allows children to choose from a bank of resources (settings, props, characters, voice-overs) and retell traditional stories or discuss social issues such as bullying or friendship as part of the PSHE curriculum.

CASE STUDY 2

A Year 4 class was organised into small groups and each group was given the task to develop a narrative using a commercial storyboarding program. They were given instructions to create a story for a group of younger children with the teacher emphasising the word 'audience'. They were also asked to develop their story in five slides. They had already created a storyboard in their class and had moved into the ICT suite to put their stories on the computer. A group of boys including two with literacy difficulties, who were usually quiet during literacy activities, and one boy with ASD (Autistic Spectrum Disorder) were working around the screen to develop their story about Alan the Alien.

Ali: *Alan should go there . . . just next to the spaceship! Look! This is where we drew him last week.*

Tom: *No! He should stay there (pointing to the tree in the setting). He has already arrived on earth and he is hiding behind the tree so the guards can't find him!*

Dennis: *Just wait a minute! Let's see what Lee wants. What do you want, Lee?*

Lee: *Alan goes there (he points to the spaceship).*

Dennis: *Do you mean next to the spaceship?*

Lee: *Yes! He is walking to the tree but he must walk from the spaceship to the tree.*

Dennis: *I think he is right. Then our audience will know that he has arrived from space.*

Tom: *. . . but we only have five slides! Lee? Can't Alan go behind the tree and we can say that he has just arrived from space?*

Lee: *I want to say it.*

Ali: *Yeah! We can say that he has just landed. (Ali pretends he is holding a spaceship that is about to land and makes the sound of the spaceship engine.)*

Dennis: *Yeah! Let's do that!*

While at an initial look it may seem that Dennis dominates the group, it is obvious that he tries to support them reach a consensus. He is aware of Lee not participating in the decision-making process and brings him in. By becoming the central person in the group he allows for others to express their points of view and move on with their story. The multimedia set-up of the program supports the engagement of the group in developing their narrative. The discussion focuses on the position of a character on the screen, which may seem like a low level cognitive activity. However, it entails creative skills as the children negotiate how they can use the features of the program to influence their story.

As part of the Speaking and Listening Programme of Study children are involved in Drama activities some of which can be supported by ICT. The British Film Institute (BFI) encourages the use of video extracts in language and literacy while tapes can be used for the children to listen to stories or music and describe emotions, characters and settings.

Programmable toys such as Roamers, Pixies or Bee-Bobs can also be used to initiate collaborative tasks and imaginative scenarios.

CASE STUDY 3

Children in a Year 2 class worked in ability groups to develop a cross-curricular activity themed 'A day in the life of a mini beast'. The children dressed up their Roamers and Bee-Bobs as their chosen mini beast, drew settings on A1 sheets of paper (the sky over a field full of flowers, a forest in spring) and programmed the toys to follow the journey of the mini beast. When they were ready, they presented their stories to the rest of the class. As they were getting ready for their presentations the teacher asked each group to prepare two questions to ask their classmates about the mini beasts' journeys. Throughout the activity the children had to work collaboratively to negotiate ideas and develop their stories. They had to decide as a group on the route that the mini beast would take, program the toys, edit and refine their decisions as they moved on. The teacher made sure that the children had clear rules for group work and the adults in the class had clear ideas of how to support the children. She went around listening to and helping individual groups when they needed some guidance. Before she moved on to the next group, she made sure that the children gained some understanding of how to move on with the task independently.

Technology also offers the possibility to simulate social situations that can be potentially dangerous or demanding for some children. Learning about road safety or social interaction can be presented in a video extract and discussed with the children at the safety of the classroom environment. The local community can also provide the stimulus and context for children's collaboration using ICT.

CASE STUDY 4

A class of 33 Year 6 mixed ability pupils were studying the ICT unit 'Graphical Modelling'. They used 'paint' software to present a graphic floor plan layout of a new local library. The children worked in carefully chosen pairs with a

---

bilingual teaching assistant supporting the lesson. The duration of the lesson in the ICT suite was one hour. The children were presented with an open-ended task with the learning objective: 'Design a new local library'.

Prior to the ICT session, the children were given around 30 minutes to draft designs on their own, after which these ideas were shared as a whole class. This ensured that the initial brainstorming and thinking process had been explored before working on the computer. Children often waste valuable ICT lesson time because their 'self-thinking' process has not been explored individually. As a result, active collaborative talk does not take place as the pairs are trying to formulate ideas for the task rather than discussing and comparing ideas. Preparation talk time is extremely valuable for generating the pace and quality of talk needed in the ICT suite. It also allows the less able and early bilingual children to feel more confident in sharing their ideas.

The children actively compared their draft paper plans in the ICT suite with their buddies. The pairs were required to collaboratively discuss and compare their designs, identifying the best design features of each plan. In order for this collaborative and exploratory talk to be effective, clear speaking and listening rules had already been established as part of the normal classroom routine, one of which was: 'To offer positive criticism'.

In order to develop critical speaking skills, the children were provided with speaking frame structures:

I like the way you included... because...
But I think... in mine is better because...
Shall we consider using... from yours and... from mine?

These speaking structures ensured the talk was focused and helped to avoid possible disagreements of a negative nature. One ICT buddy pair worked particularly well where an able Gujarati/English speaking child supported a less able Gujarati speaking child. Key phrases and nouns were translated and explained by the more fluent child. It is vital that knowledge is not equated to thinking capacity as this leads to low expectations of early bilingual learners where often language is the only key barrier.

Through collaborative discussion the pairs created inspiring designs with a variety of interesting furniture features. The discussions were lively, yet the talk was clearly focused around the task; the use of ICT allowing the children to quickly make changes on the plan and explore alternative furniture layouts. One pair was asked by the teacher:

- Why have you placed all the bookshelves so close together?
- How would visitors feel in that area?
- What if you moved/re-organised certain shelves to other areas of the library?
- What effect would this have?

Working 'in role' as designers provided the children with the elevated status of imagined real-life professionals. As a result, the talk generated was focused, constructive and the task provided opportunities for genuine collaboration.

Supporting teachers' practice in organising speaking and listening activities

ICT can support teachers in preparing whole-class activities that they can share on the interactive whiteboard which have become an integral part of the teaching and learning environment in many schools. A summary of research evidence by Becta (2003b) emphasises that, compared to other ICT resources, interactive whiteboards present more opportunities for teachers and children to interact and discuss in the classroom.

A recent lesson with Year 3 children demonstrated how the teacher made effective use of the potential of the whiteboard software by incorporating the 'Hide and Reveal' feature. The teacher uploaded the painting *Beach Scene* by Degas taken from the National Portrait Gallery (www.takeonepicture.com) on the whiteboard and began by disclosing a small segment of the painting. The children were asked to look at the image individually and hypothesise about what was going on and where the picture was set and then share their ideas within a group context, justifying their responses. The images of shivering children inspired the children to generate a narrative in which people were fleeing from a catastrophe such as a fire in the middle of the night. Different sections of the painting were then revealed on the whiteboard which required children to reshape their ideas and their interpretations of the image they were seeing. The gradual revelation of the images to the whole picture generated excitement and enthusiasm among the children and provided the focus for the discussion. The teacher's role was to support the children's language development by providing key words and phrases suggested by the picture. The activity provided opportunities for the children to:

- interrogate their own understanding;
- generate ideas;
- explain and instruct;
- argue a personal point of view;
- reach a consensus.

ICT can be a very powerful means of influencing the kind of talk that goes on in the classroom, particularly the relationship between teacher and pupil talk. The Literacy Hour presented a very teacher-centred, didactic model of teaching where the teacher initiated discussion, children responded and received feedback on their answers. The interpretation of the word 'pace' often led to very short interchanges where sustained responses or initiatives from the children which detracted from the learning objectives were not encouraged. Work by Robin Alexander (2004) advocates an approach where children and teachers consider learning tasks in a more open and discursive way, an approach he calls 'dialogic teaching' (see Chapter 1).

When organising ICT activities the teachers can consider what opportunities they offer the pupils to develop effective dialogic relationships in the classroom. The dynamic relationships between the pupil and the technology need to be supported by the teacher who will be able to structure relevant activities and help pupils develop understanding and independence. This is particularly important with some ICT applications. For instance, developing criteria in evaluating the content of websites and selecting relevant information are crucial skills that pupils need to demonstrate in KS2.

Planning for communicative ICT activities

Research into speaking and listening[12] emphasises the need for teachers to plan rigorously and provide structured opportunities for the effective teaching of talk. In so doing, it is vital to build on children's previous experience, both in terms of ICT and in speaking and listening. Figure 10.1 presents the stages that you can consider when organising an ICT activity.

Corden[13] also discusses the importance of developing clearly structured teacher–pupil interaction in establishing successful computer-based talk. He summarises findings from research literature on computers and group work that were produced the early 1990s. These findings highlighted the importance of teacher interventions during the ICT activity. He comments that the task also needs to be based on clear aims, objectives and ground rules for group work, points that are still relevant in maintaining worthwhile ICT learning experiences. Furthermore, Ofsted (2002) have identified that the most effective use of ICT is when there is a clear literacy focus (learning intention) and the ICT clearly matches the lesson objective. They also state that teachers have a tendency to 'spoon feed' children in terms of using ICT and do not allow them to develop independence in using ICT.

Another feature of effective group work and interaction using ICT involves setting up clear roles for the group. For instance, in the digital video project described at the opening of the chapter the four children were clear about their contributions in the shooting: one of them was the director, the other one the camera person while the rest of the group were actors introducing the parts of the school. In another digital video project with a Year 6 class the children worked in groups of ten: eight of them were involved in the shooting (director, camera person, two main characters and four extras) while the other two were

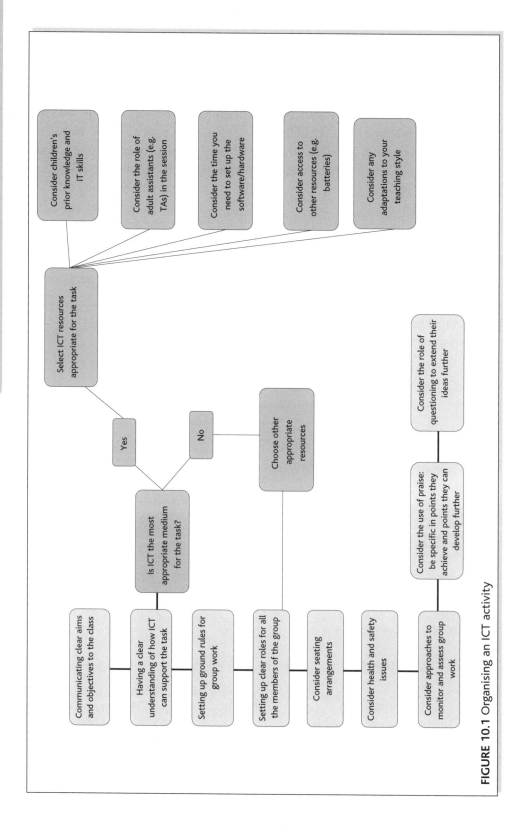

FIGURE 10.1 Organising an ICT activity

evaluators following the film crew around and making notes on PC tablets of what went well and how they can improve the clip. When the group watched the clip, the evaluators feed back to them and as a group they decided whether there were scenes that they needed to film again.

When planning for an ICT activity, it is necessary to consider how the selected software can promote collaborative learning and provide appropriate contexts for speaking and listening. The following points are adapted from Wegerif's work (undated) and provide some starting points in making decisions about selecting a program:

- Does the software present meaningful challenges and problems for the children?
- Do these challenges provide a range of alternative choices for discussion?
- Does the software offer a clear purpose or task which is made evident to the group and kept in focus throughout?
- Are there on-screen prompts which remind the children to talk together, reach agreement and ask for opinions and reasons?
- Does it provide resources for discussion and opportunities to review decisions in the light of new information?
- Does it have features which encourage children to take turns, beat the clock or encourage competitive ways of working which detract from effective collaborative learning and exploratory talk?

Organising an ICT activity also involves considering the learning space and how this contributes to the development of the task. We need to be aware of the school's policy of computer use along with health and safety issues related to the use of computers and other digital devices. We should also take into account how assistive technology that some of the children need to use will be supported during the activity. We can involve the teaching assistants, who may be in the class, as to how they could help the children during the activity.

Table 10.2 suggests some final points that can be considered when planning for an ICT activity.

Some final thoughts

The chapter has discussed how ICT can support a range of speaking and listening activities and has considered examples of classroom practice. The importance of addressing the pedagogical aims and appropriateness of technology as starting points for speaking and listening activities has been emphasised. Speaking and listening have been explored within the broader framework of communication. This is particularly relevant within the current context where the QCA English 21

Table 10.2 Considerations for planning ICT

ICT considerations	Speaking and listening considerations
• Will the children be able to work independently or will they need the support of an adult throughout? • What limitations for group work does the classroom/ICT suite present and how can you overcome them? • What is the children's prior knowledge of the activity and what are their IT skills? • Can the activity be differentiated for different abilities? Can it engage and motivate all children (taking into consideration cultural, gender differences)? • How are we going to monitor the development of the work? • What is the role of the teaching assistant or other adults who will be in the classroom?	• What kind of talk will this activity facilitate? • What contexts will the children be working in (pairs/groups)? • How will the groups be organised? Who will choose? • Have children had the opportunity to work in groups before? • Are ground rules for group discussion and interaction needed? • What shared metalanguage will be needed? • How are we going to measure success?

initiative is inviting discussion on the redefinition of the term 'English'. One response suggests that 'a more holistic approach to teaching [is necessary] which integrates speaking and listening with the use of new technologies'.[14] This chapter has identified successful areas of current practice and a clear rationale for developing ICT within language and literacy teaching.

Notes

1. Becta (2003b). Available at: http://www.becta.org.uk/research/research.cfm?section=1&id=546
2. Theodosakis (2002).
3. Dimitriadi and Hodson (2004).
4. Hennessey *et al.* (2003).
5. DfES (2003a) Every Child Matters Green Paper. Available at: http://www.dfes.gov.uk/everychildmatters
6. Reid *et al.* (2002).
7. Bearne, E. 'Texts and Technologies'. Available at: http://www.qca.org.uk/11782_11909.html
8. Livingstone and Bober (2004).
9. Prensky (2001); Facer (2003).
10. Abbott (2002).
11. Mercer and Wegerif (1998).
12. Cormack, Wignall and Hughes (1998) *Classroom Discourse Project.* Available at: http://www.griffithedu.au/schools/cls/clearinghouse/1998_classroom/cal.pdf

13. Corden (2002).
14. UKLA (2005) *Response to QCA's English 21 Initiative.* Available at:
    http://www.ukla.org/site/publications/papers/7.php

References and further reading

Abbott, C. (2002) 'Making the Internet Special', in C. Abbott (ed.) *Special Educational Needs and the Internet.* London: RoutledgeFalmer.

Becta (2003a) Entitlement to ICT in Primary English. Available at: http://www.ictadvice.org.uk/

Becta (2003b) *What the Research Says About Digital Video in Teaching and Learning.* Coventry: Becta. Available at: http://www.becta.org.uk/research/research.cfm?section=1&id=546

Birmingham, P. and Davies, C. (2001) 'Storyboarding Shakespeare: learners' interactions with storyboard software in the process of understanding difficult literacy texts', *Journal of Information Technology for Teacher Education,* 10(3): 241–53.

Corden, R. (2002) 'Learning through talk', in T. Grainger (ed.) (2004) *The RoutledgeFalmer Reader in Language and Literacy.* London: RoutledgeFalmer.

Cormack, P., Wignall, P. and Nichols, S. (1998) *Classroom Discourse Project.* Available at: http://www.griffithedu.au/schools/cls/clearinghouse/1998_classroom/cal.pdf

DfEE (1999) *The National Curriculum for ICT.* London: DfEE.

DfES (2003a) Every Child Matters Green Paper. Available at: http://www.dfes.gov.uk/everychildmatters

DfES (2003b) *Excellence and Enjoyment: A Strategy for Primary Schools.* London: DfES.

DfES (2003c) *Speaking, Listening, Learning: Working with Children in Key Stages 1 and 2.* London: DfES.

Dimitriadi, Y. and Hodson, P. (2004) *Digital Video and Bilingual Children with Special Educational Needs: Supporting Literacy Activities.* Available at: http://www.becta.org.uk/research/reports/digitalvideo/

Hennessey, S. *et al.* (2003) *Pedagogic Strategies for Using ICT to Support Subject Teaching and Learning: An Analysis Across 15 Case Studies.* Cambridge: University of Cambridge Faculty of Education, Research Report no. 03/1.

Higgins, S. and Moseley, D. (2002) 'Raising achievement in literacy through ICT', in M. Monteith (ed.) *Teaching Primary Literacy with ICT.* Maidenhead: Open University Press.

Livingstone, S. and Bober, M. (2004) *UK Children Go Online. Surveying the Experiences of Young People and Their Parents.* London: Department of Media and Communications, The London School of Economics and Political Science.

Mercer, N. and Wegerif, R. (1998) 'Is "exploratory talk" productive talk?', in K. Littleton and P. Light. *Learning with Computers: Analysing Productive Interaction.* New York: Routledge.

Prensky, M. (2001) *On the Horizon.* NCB University Press, Vol. 9, No. 5.

Reid, M. *et al.* (2002) *Evaluation of the Becta Digital Video Pilot Project.* Coventry: Becta.

Sharpe, J., Potter, J., Allen, J. and Loveless, A. (2002) ICT in Teacher Education. Exeter: Learning Matters.

Theodosakis, N. (2002) *How Digital Filmmaking Develops Higher-Order Thinking Skills.* VSTE. Available at: http://www.vste.org.uk

UKLA (2005) *Response to QCA's English 21 Initiative.* Available at: http://www.ukla.org/site/publications/papers/7.php

Virtual Teacher Centre (2003) ICT and the English Curriculum. Available at: http://vtc.ngfl.gov.uk/docserver.php?temid=84

Index